Reading Fluency and Comprehension Activities & Exercises™

by Nancy B. Swigert

D1560851

Skills

- reading fluency
- vocabulary
- comprehension

Ages

- 6 through 14

Grades

- 1 through 8

Evidence-Based Practice

According to the Preferred Practice Patterns and other documents of The American Speech-Language-Hearing Association (www.asha.org) and the National Reading Panel, *Teaching Children to Read: An Evidence-Based Assessment of the Scientific Research Literature on Reading and Its Implications for Reading Instruction— Reports of the Subgroups* (www.nichd.nih.gov/publications/nrp/report, 2000), and the National Institute For Literacy, National Institute for Child Health and Development, Partnership for Reading (www.nifl.gov/ partnershipforreading/explore/fluency.html) the following therapy principles are supported:

- Providing instruction of vocabulary words prior to reading can facilitate both vocabulary acquisition and reading comprehension.

- Repeated and monitored oral reading improves fluency and overall reading achievement.

- Oral reading practice leads to an improvement in reading fluency.

- Research shows that reading comprehension improves when a combination of techniques are used such as question answering, question generation, and summarization.

- Intervention targets the most intact level at which success can be achieved (although skills may be isolated for concentrated practice).

- Decoding activities alone are not enough, but should be implemented hand-in-hand with fluency-building activities (e.g., guided repeated readings, increased time spent in reading).

- Activities should be designed specifically to teach students with special needs to apply new knowledge and skills in functional contexts for authentic reading, writing, listening, speaking, and thinking purposes.

- Intervention goals and objectives are reviewed periodically to determine continued appropriateness.

- In working with students from a variety of cultural backgrounds, it is important to use culturally relevant reading and writing materials and tasks.

The tasks in this book incorporate the above principles and are also based on expert professional practice.

LinguiSystems

LinguiSystems, Inc.
3100 4th Avenue
East Moline, IL 61244-9700
800-776-4332

FAX: 800-577-4555
E-mail: service@linguisystems.com
Web: linguisystems.com

Copyright © 2006 LinguiSystems, Inc.

Printed in the U.S.A.
ISBN 0-7606-0690-0

About the Author

Nancy B. Swigert, M.A., CCC-SLP, is president of Swigert & Associates, Inc., a private practice that has been providing services in the Lexington, Kentucky area for over 25 years. She also serves as president of the Reading Center, a program that provides assessment and intervention for children and adults with reading, spelling, and written language disorders. She has provided training and consultation for numerous private and public school systems concerning these disorders. The Reading Center is an approved provider of supplemental educational services for the No Child Left Behind initiative. Nancy is the author of five other books for LinguiSystems: *The Source for Dysphagia, The Source for Dysarthria, The Source for Pediatric Dysphagia, The Source for Children's Voice Disorders,* and *The Source for Reading Fluency.* She is very active in the American Speech-Language-Hearing Association, including serving as its president in 1998. She was also president of the American Speech-Language-Hearing Foundation in 2004 and 2005.

Acknowledgments

Completing a book is never a solo effort. Such a task is accomplished with the capable assistance of several individuals at Swigert & Associates, Inc.

Thanks to:

- Geri Cadle, Executive Assistant, for monitoring timelines, coordinating staff, and careful editing

- Melinda Spurlock for organizing references; finding books at the library; and counting, counting, counting words!

- Lacey Graves for helping develop some of the activities and formatting others

- June Ballman for reorganizing all the materials after we've used them and completing any other task that needed to be done

Edited by Kelly Malone
Cover design by Chris Claus
Page layout design by Lisa M. Parker
Page layout by Denise L. Kelly and Jamie Bellagamba

Table of Contents

Introduction

One of the main challenges we continue to face at the Reading Center is helping children become fluent readers. These are the students who, despite improvements in their phonological awareness skills and applied decoding skills, still can't read quickly enough and well enough to keep up with their grade-level peers.

What we saw at our center was not unique. Reading rate is a significant problem for children with reading problems. The National Reading Panel report (2000) indicated that 44% of fourth graders were non-fluent readers. The National Assessment of Educational Progress (NAEP) study (Johnson, E.G. et al., 1992) found that 15% of all fourth graders (1 out of 7) read "no faster than 74 words per minute . . . a pace at which it would be difficult to keep track of ideas as they are developing within the sentence and across the page." They also found that the below-basic readers (about 40%) did not differ from basic and above-average readers in their accuracy, but their rate was significantly lower than those two other groups. The oral reading rate was highly correlated to students' comprehension on a silent reading of that text (Pinnell et al., 1995). Students have to read 130 words correct per minute (WCPM) to be proficient on assessments like the NAEP at the fourth-grade level (Pinnell et al., 1995).

Lovett's observations (1987) mirror our own—children with reading rate disorders tend to be referred by the time they reach the middle and later elementary grades. This is when the amount of textual information they're required to manage for test and project preparation increases and when instruction is more in lecture format.

In addition to the close tie that has been established between reading fluency and comprehension, it has been suggested that dysfluent reading also affects the reader's motivation to read (Meyer & Felton, 1999). This is not surprising if you listen to a non-fluent reader read. He certainly must find reading to be extremely frustrating and laborious. This may cause him to avoid reading at all costs.

The Matthews principle (Stanovich, 1986) states that better readers read more, and thus, continue to improve. Reading progress is largely dependent on how much reading the person does. Slow, inefficient readers read fewer words per minute. Thus, they would have to read many more hours just to keep up with their peers in amount of text read.

Working with students with reading fluency problems prompted me to research the theory behind fluency in reading and compile and develop materials to help these students. The results of that research and work culminated in *The Source for Reading Fluency* (Swigert, 2003) which contains information on what reading fluency is and how to test for it as well as many practice activities and resources for helping students become fluent readers.

These activities and resources address areas such as:

▶ Recognition of letter, syllable, and word patterns
▶ Recognition of sight words
▶ Efficient decoding skills
▶ Improved word retrieval
▶ Semantics and vocabulary
▶ Increased reading in connected text

I have heard from many people who find *The Source for Reading Fluency* useful and want more practice materials to use with these students. *Reading Fluency and Comprehension: Activities & Exercises* is the result of listening to those requests.

Reading Fluency and Comprehension: Activities & Exercises is divided into seven chapters and focuses on activities to improve reading fluency (accuracy and speed) in connected text in three main ways:

1 Passages to use with repeat reading
2 Activities for improving attention to the details in text
3 Practice responding to prosodic and syntactic cues

Chapter 1 reviews the information from *The Source for Reading Fluency* on what reading fluency is.

Chapter 2 explains the methods for which practice materials are provided. Here you'll find information on repeat reading. There is also information about activities to increase accuracy in connected text and a summary of the impact of prosody and syntax on fluency.

Chapter 3 highlights reading comprehension and the importance of integrating work on comprehension with fluency.

Chapter 4 describes the challenges and pitfalls to readability formulae used to determine grade level of reading material.

Chapter 5 contains graded passages for repeat reading for grades 1–8 as well as forms needed to track student progress and handouts to explain the technique to parents. These passages also contain questions to improve comprehension.

Chapter 6 contains activities for increasing accuracy and increasing attention to prosody and syntax.

Chapter 7 describes other resources available to address reading fluency.

Is another book on reading fluency really needed? In a study analyzing the predictive value of rapid automatized naming in poor readers, Meyer et al. (1998) stated, "the practical consequences of these findings argue for increased emphasis on instructional techniques that stress fluency training in the early grades."

I couldn't agree more. Reading fluency work shouldn't wait until the fourth or fifth grade. Readers in late first grade or early second grade should be fluent on grade level materials. I hope that you find the information and materials in this book useful as you strive to help the non-fluent readers you know to become more fluent.

Nancy

Fluent readers can read text quickly and accurately. In addition, fluent readers read with expression, enhancing the understandability of the passage. There is a noticeable and recognizable difference between a fluent reader and a non-fluent reader. Think of the difference in how you sound when you read aloud from a familiar children's book. Compare that to how you would sound if you were to read an unfamiliar text on quantum physics. In the latter situation, you might be able to read the words, but you probably wouldn't do so fluently.

Fluent reading might be described as a "lack of trouble with word identification or comprehension" (Leu & Kinzer, 1987). A similar definition is found in *A Dictionary of Reading and Related Terms* (Harris & Hodges, 1981) as "freedom from word identification problems." Picture the student who reads fluently as being able to read while not being tied to a word-by-word or sound-by-sound process.

Fluent readers
▶ **Quick**
▶ **Accurate**
▶ **Attend to punctuation**
▶ **Use expression**
rhythm
intonation
phrasing

Hook and Jones (2002) indicate that fluency involves not only automatic word recognition but also the ability to attend to prosodic features (e.g., rhythm, intonation, phrasing) at the phrase, sentence, and text level. Wood et al. (2001) state that fluency also involves anticipation of what comes next in the text. This anticipation facilitates reaction time and aids comprehension.

LaBerge and Samuels (1974) were early advocates of the idea that it is not enough to achieve accuracy in reading. They stated that fluent reading is achieved only when all levels from visual to semantic decoding occur automatically. Samuels (1992) explains that reading requires decoding, comprehension, and attention. Readers cannot achieve fluent reading with good comprehension if their attention is focused on decoding. Once decoding becomes automatic, attention can be focused on comprehension. It is at that point that the reader has become fluent.

Beginning readers are rarely fluent readers. Their attention is focused on individual letters and sounds and on decoding these to figure out what the word is. As readers develop skill, they focus on larger and larger units (e.g., digraphs and word parts). When the student is a fluent reader, the unit of focus is the whole word (Samuels, 1992).

The relationship between decoding and comprehension

As the student progresses towards fluency, less and less of his mental energy, or attention, has to be focused on the decoding process. This means that he can begin to focus his attention on comprehending what he is reading.

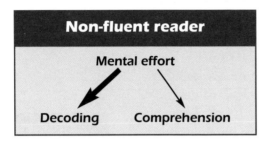
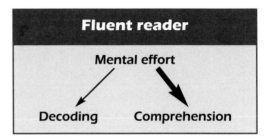

Samuels (1992) states, "The hallmark of fluent reading is the ability to decode and comprehend at the same time." Different studies have exhibited that, in general, less fluent readers have poorer comprehension (Carnine et al., 1990; Dowhower, 1987; Shinn et al., 1992; Tan & Nicholson, 1997). For that reason, I have included activities to address both fluency and comprehension in this book.

Perfetti and Lesgold (1977) described the relationship between decoding and comprehension as the bottleneck hypothesis. If decoding is not fast and accurate, then there will be a bottleneck for comprehension. This is because coding operations may share what these authors call the "limited capacity processor" with comprehension. Rather than calling it *mental effort* or *energy*, they refer to it as *memory*. They indicate that the limited capacity processor can only hold so much information in memory.

Automaticity

The term *automaticity* is often used in descriptions of reading fluency. A task is described as automatic when it can be completed without overt attention. Berninger et al. (2001) differentiate between efficiency (speed) and automaticity (direct access). When you finished reading the paragraph above, did you have any recollection of decoding any specific word? Without that overt attention to decoding, you still comprehended what you read. You have reached the level of automaticity in reading, allowing you to focus your attention on comprehending the content. If you are able to do two tasks at once, decoding and comprehending, then one of those tasks has become automatic (Samuels, 1992). Samuels points out that automaticity is not achieved simply by reaching an automatic level for decoding. He points out that other "text processing strategies" also have to run automatically. These might include being able to visualize the text, understand a referent, or understand the structure of the text. The relationship between fluency and comprehension is not one-way. The more you understand what you are reading, the more fluent you can be when reading the text.

Shiffrin and Schneider (1977) explained automatic behaviors in terms of features and outcomes of those behaviors. They described automatic behaviors as:

▶ Being difficult to inhibit
▶ Not relying on conscious control and attention
▶ Not utilizing attentional resources when the individual is performing them at the same time as another task

Nasland and Smolkin (1997) concluded, "Reading . . . (is) a skill that develops to a more automatic level depending on the degree to which the individual can accurately and quickly access phonemic and lexical representations . . .."

Think of non-reading tasks that you may perform automatically. If you drive a standard shift car, you probably reach the end of your journey with no recollection of how often or when you had to shift. If you engage in needlework (e.g., knitting or needlepoint), you can probably do this while completing another task, such as talking with a friend or watching TV. If you had to think about each and every stitch you took, needlework wouldn't be much fun. Reading is similar in the need to reach automaticity. If reading is too much work, our students won't want to read. We shouldn't be satisfied when they can read a sentence and correctly decode the words. We should strive to have the student read the material quickly and smoothly.

The double-deficit hypothesis

Why are some children slow readers? What underlying processes are impaired? Perhaps the best-known work is that done by Wolf and Bowers. They first described their theory on the links between naming speed, timing, and orthographic skills in 1993. In their seminal paper on naming speed deficits (Wolf & Bowers, 1999), they explained that it had long been believed that a core deficit in phonological processes impedes the acquisition of word recognition skills, which, in turn, impedes the acquisition of fluent reading. They further stated many severely-impaired readers have naming-speed deficits (i.e., deficits in the processes underlying the rapid recognition and retrieval of visually presented linguistic stimuli). Their double-deficit hypothesis proposed, however, that the naming-speed deficit was not part of impaired phonological processes but instead that "Phonological deficits and the processes underlying naming speed are separable sources of reading dysfunction, and their combined presence leads to profound reading impairment."

Other authors have confirmed the double-deficit theory by isolating reading skills that are more directly related to naming speed than to phonological awareness skills. Cornwall (1992) showed that rapid letter naming added significantly to the prediction of word identification, prose passage speed, and accuracy scores. Manis and Freedman (2001) obtained several findings relevant to the theory.

They found that phonological skills and rapid serial naming made differential contributions to particular aspects of word reading skill. They further found that rapid automatic naming (RAN) was most strongly predictive of accuracy and latency measures of orthographic and semantic processing, and latency measures of word and non-word reading. Manis et al. (1999) suggest that this differential effect on reading may be because RAN involves arbitrary associations between print and sound (e.g., a letter and its name). They suggest that phoneme awareness is more related to the student learning a systematic spelling-sound correspondence. In addition, they state that RAN has a number of other components that overlap with reading and make it a good predictor of reading skills.

Manis et al. (2000) confirmed naming speed's contribution to measures of orthographic skill compared to phonemic awareness's stronger contribution to non-word decoding. Torgeson et al. (1997) showed unique contributions of both phonemic awareness and naming speed in predicting second and third grade reading when measured in kindergarten and first grade.

Reading skills related to naming speed
▶ Word identification ▶ Word reading speed ▶ Passage accuracy

What the double-deficit theory means for treatment

Why is it important to consider the theory of separable sources (phonological deficits and processes underlying naming speed deficits) of reading dysfunction? It is important because how a disorder is viewed shapes the way it is treated. If the processes underlying naming speed deficits are really just one of the phonological processes that can be impaired, then the majority of children with reading disorders would be well served by improving their phonological awareness skills. However, if Wolf and Bower's double-deficit theory is accurate and the processes underlying naming speed deficits are indeed a separate source of reading dysfunction, then to treat all children with reading disorders in the same way would be inappropriate and probably not productive for those children with naming speed deficits.

This has indeed been demonstrated in several studies (Lovett et al., 1994). Lovett found significant differences in the effectiveness of her program. Specifically, the phonological-deficit-only group showed greater gains on every post-treatment measure than either the naming-speed or the double-deficit group. Some of these measures were phonological processing, non-word and word identification skill, and standardized reading measures. The conclusion was that phonological intervention can help some children with reading disabilities, but some groups of readers have a deficit pattern that will require additional or different emphases in intervention.

Children with deficits in the processes underlying naming speed need specific strategies and techniques to try to improve those processes. Children with phonological awareness deficits need techniques to improve their phonological awareness skills. If the child has deficits in both phonological awareness and naming speed, then that child suffers from what Wolf and Bowers describe as a *double deficit*. For those children, it is crucial that a combined approach be utilized. Treatment must address their reduced phonological process skills and the processes underlying their naming-speed deficit.

Naming-speed deficit and reading

How does an impairment in the processes underlying naming speed result in slow reading? Wolf and Bowers have indicated that there may be three ways this may occur:

1 Impeding connections between phonemes and the orthographic patterns at word or sub-word levels

2 Limiting the quality of the orthographic codes stored in memory

3 Requiring increased practice before adequate connections are made

Wolf and Bowers' theoretical description of how processes underlying naming speed result in slow reading implies that intervention needs to:

▶ Help the student improve the connections between phonemes and their orthographic patterns and between word parts and words and their orthographic patterns. Intervention must not only focus on the phonemic level but also on helping students improve the speed of recognition of word parts (e.g., onsets and rimes, prefixes and suffixes) and whole words. These connections must occur rapidly and without conscious thought on the part of the student.

▶ Help the student improve the quality of orthographic codes he is able to hold in memory. Often the student knows many of the basic codes (e.g., short and long vowels) but does not have other orthographic codes stored (e.g., alternative spellings for the long *e* such as *ea*, what a blend says: *spr*).

▶ Provide the student ample practice to help these connections become automatic.

Wolf and Bowers stress helping the student improve speed and accuracy of connections. Apel and Swank (1999) describe these connections as establishing visual orthographic images (VOI). These are mental images of morphemes, syllables, or words that are developed in memory by repeated successful experiences in decoding words. These authors indicate that in normally-developing readers, as little as four exposures to a word may be needed to establish a VOI. Once this image of a morpheme, syllable, or word is established, the reader can bypass the slower act of decoding. In children with impaired naming speed, many more exposures to a pattern may be needed.

Word recognition and fluency

Word recognition is crucial in the beginning reader. Early readers learn to recognize the word as a unit. One of the challenges for beginning readers is to understand how these written forms map onto their oral vocabulary. Deficits in word level recognition have been shown to be characteristic of students who are not reading at grade level (Perfetti, 1985; Stanovich, 1986). Still others state, "The development of rapid word recognition skills . . . (is) the primary factor which distinguishes skilled from less skilled reading performance" (Chabot et al., 1984).

Several theories describe how word recognition develops (Coltheart, 1978; Forster, 1976; LaBerge & Samuels, 1974; McClelland & Rumelhart, 1981; Seidenberg & McClelland, 1989). At least some of those models recognize that a "framework assumes that reading words involves the computation of three types of codes: orthographic, phonological, and semantic" (Seidenberg & McClelland, 1989).

When do readers begin to establish VOIs of morphemes and word parts to decode words? Some say that children as young as six or seven may tap their emerging knowledge of morphemes for written language (Treiman & Cassar, 1997). By fourth grade, students seem to have a basic knowledge of derived forms (Windson & Hwang, 1997) and by fifth grade, a substantial portion of the child's orthographic representations consist of forms that are derivations of root words (Anglin, 1993).

Semantics and fluency

Achieving reading fluency would seem to depend not just on enhancing connections for more efficient orthographic and phonological processing but also on more efficient use of semantics. In their work developing *Retrieval, Automaticity, Vocabulary Elaboration, and Orthography (RAVE-O)* (a comprehensive, fluency-based reading intervention program), Wolf et al. (2000) indicate that it is also important to improve the student's semantic knowledge. They state that dysfluent readers cannot afford the time to process different meanings of a word they have read. If students have a rich vocabulary with easy access to multiple meanings of words, they will be able to more quickly retrieve this information during reading. This will help to improve the speed of reading. Obviously, understanding the meaning of words is also crucial to comprehension.

Fluency in connected reading

Attention to all the skills that contribute to fluent reading is important, but we must also help the student apply these skills with the result being increased speed and fluency of connected reading. This involves practice with oral reading, word level drills, and increasing attention to prosodic cues. It is important to remember that when treating component parts, the goal is ultimately to help the student read connected text more fluently.

Are there subtypes of non-fluent readers?

It is likely that we may determine that naming-speed deficit is more complex as we learn more about it. If the model of naming-speed deficit is more complex than that described previously, then how intervention is provided would also be more complex. Berninger et al. (2001) elaborate on the concept of naming-speed deficit and indicate they have observed three subtypes of dysfluent readers.

Type 1: Processing Rate/Efficiency Impaired
Type 2: Automaticity Impaired
Type 3: Executive Coordination Impaired

Within each of these three subtypes, different processes may be contributing to slow oral reading. In addition, Beringer et al. hypothesize that there is a different brain locus for each of the types. A summary of their description of oral reading in children in each of these subtypes follows.

Processing rate or efficiency of the system
Oral reading is very accurate but painfully slow in children who are processing rate or efficiency impaired. These children rarely make errors and thus are often not identified by schools as having a reading disability. These are the children who may not be able to keep up with assignments in the classroom. The hypothesized brain locus is the cerebellum, for control of precise timing.

Automaticity of processing
Oral reading is inaccurate and slow with very specific types of errors in children who are automaticity impaired. Errors include false starts, hesitations that are often filled with pauses, and repetitions. These children seem to have adequate phonological awareness skills but have not achieved an automatic level of processing. They do seem able to self-monitor and self-correct. Berninger et al. suggest that this means the children's executive functions are intact. They propose the brain locus for this type of deficit to be the striatum and/or insula.

Executive coordination
The third subtype described by Berninger et al. exhibits oral reading that is inaccurate and slow but has an error pattern different from that in the second subtype. These children make errors indicating an "inattention to orthographic and morphological features of words, inattention to serial order of words in sentences, inattention to the prosody or music of the language (Erekson, 1999), and inattention to self-monitoring of meaning." They rarely self-correct errors. Berninger et al. hypothesize the brain locus is left frontal for this type of deficit.

Berninger et al. note that some children exhibit errors characteristic of Types 2 and 3, and they indicate this means that both automaticity and executive coordination are affected. It would seem that these children would have even more difficulty becoming fluent readers. At the Reading Center, we have found that most children exhibit a combination of errors characteristic of Type 2 and 3, while few are the ploddingly slow readers of Type 1. Perhaps that is more reflective of the types of children referred to our center than to the distribution of these types across non-fluent readers.

Others describe a different categorization for the types of non-fluent readers. Children described as the guessing subtype of dyslexia are those who read fast and inaccurately, while children with the spelling subtype of dyslexia read slowly and accurately. This latter type of dyslexia, spelling subtype, would mirror Berninger et al.'s Type 1. The guessing subtype of dyslexia probably most closely reflects Berninger et al.'s Type 3 description.

Would different subtypes need different treatment?

If we accept Berninger et al.'s more detailed breakdown of types of dysfluent readers, then we must also adjust the intervention provided. They suggest that students in the first subtype may need work mostly on practicing reading to increase efficiency; however, the second type may need to improve the connections between stimuli and responses and need feedback on their rate and accuracy during reading. Finally, the third type may need instruction in meta-cognitive strategies for self-monitoring and self-correction.

Conclusion

Because the concept of fluency in reading and the relationship to processes underlying naming speed is complex and relatively recent, research continues to yield much new information. The current working definition of fluency provided by Wolf and Katzir-Cohen (2001) summarizes well our current understanding:

"In its beginnings, reading fluency is the product of the initial development of accuracy and the subsequent development of automaticity in underlying sublexical processes, lexical processes, and their integration in single-word reading and connected text. These include perceptual, phonological, orthographic, and morphological processes at the letter, letter-pattern, and word levels, as well as semantic and syntactic processes at the word level and connected-text level. After it is fully developed, reading fluency refers to a level of accuracy and rate where decoding is relatively effortless, where oral reading is smooth and accurate with correct prosody, and where attention can be allocated to comprehension."

We know a non-fluent reader when we hear one. The challenge is to determine how we can help that reader become more fluent. The handout on pages 15-16 may help you explain the concept of reading fluency to parents and teachers.

14

Children who are fluent readers can read material with speed, accuracy, and proper expression. Allington (1983) described fluency as the most neglected reading skill. In 1995, the National Assessment of Educational Progress conducted a large study of the status of fluency achievement in a representative sample of fourth graders (Pinnell et al., 1995). This study found 44% of students to be dysfluent even with grade-level stories that students read under supportive testing conditions. This study also found a close relationship between how fluently the children read and their comprehension.

Why would problems with reading accuracy, speed, and expression interfere with comprehension?

Think of the reading process as two basic cognitive tasks. The reader must:

1 Recognize the printed words
2 Derive meaning from the recognized words (comprehension)

These tasks require cognitive resources, of which there is a limited supply. If the child expends too much cognitive effort on recognizing the word, there is little left for deriving meaning. This results in reading being a slow, laborious process.

The importance of word recognition skills

To be a fluent reader, the child needs to have good word recognition skills. Word recognition involves both accuracy and automaticity of word recognition. To help develop these skills, children need to improve the speed of some underlying processes for word recognition. These include the ability to:

✓ Retrieve and recognize phonological patterns—what they look like, sound like, and feel like when they are pronounced

✓ Recognize written letter patterns (e.g., word endings and beginnings, consonant blends, certain spelling expectancies)

✓ Recognize auditory similarities and differences in words (e.g., words differing only by initial or final phonemes, rime patterns)

✓ Recognize common, high-frequency sight words

✓ Retrieve a specific word from vocabulary (the "tip of the tongue" phenomenon)

✓ Understand multiple meanings of words (e.g., block, duck, jam)

Understand word roots and associated words (e.g., *head* as in *headlight, headset,* and *header*) to improve storage and retrieval

 See a multisyllabic word as a group of word parts that can be recognized

What else is needed to become a fluent reader?

Good word recognition skills alone will not make the child a fluent reader. Fluency is a level of expertise beyond word recognition and accuracy. Children who do not develop reading fluency, even though they are intelligent, will continue to struggle with reading. They will read slowly, and reading will require a lot of effort. In addition to improved word recognition skills, fluency also seems to develop from reading practice.

Why would reading practice help improve fluency?

Any new act you learn requires a lot of time and close attention when you first begin to perform it. Think about learning a golf swing or a dance step. When first learning that act, you must concentrate on it a lot. The more times you repeat the movement, the more you can free your mind from the details and the more "fluent" you become. This happens with reading as well.

The National Reading Panel (December, 2000) conducted a review of the literature and drew the following conclusions:

▶ Guided, repeated oral reading improves word recognition, fluency, and comprehension.

▶ Having children read silently has not been demonstrated to increase reading fluency.

Repeated oral reading with feedback and instruction seems to be the most helpful strategy to improve fluency. Part of the instruction is helping the child recognize and respond to punctuation (e.g., knowing when to pause to improve expression and comprehension). We can provide more specific instructions on repeat reading.

References

Allington, R.L. (1983). Fluency: The neglected reading goal in reading instruction. *The Reading Teacher, 36,* 556-561.

National Reading Panel (December 2000). *Teaching children to read: An evidence-based assessment of the scientific research literature on reading and its implications for reading instruction—reports of the subgroups.* Washington, D.C.: U.S. Department of Health and Human Services, National Institute of Child Health and Development, Publication No. 00-4754.

Pinnell, G.S., Pikulski, J.J., Wixson, K.K., Campbell, J.R., Gough, P.B., & Beatty, A.S. (1995). *Listening to children read aloud.* Washington, D.C.: U.S. Department of Education, Office of Educational Research and Improvement.

Chapter 1
Reading Fluency and Comprehension   **16**

The ultimate goal of reading intervention is to assure that the student understands what she has read and can read things in a reasonable amount of time. Improving fluency of connected text reading will not only result in a faster rate of reading, but it will improve comprehension as well. This should result in improved efficiency of reading. This will permit the student to complete school assignments accurately and in a reasonable amount of time.

The Source for Reading Fluency (Swigert, 2003) describes the comprehensive nature of activities and strategies needed to work on improving reading fluency. It identifies the following areas and provides practice activities for each:

▶ Building automaticity with phonological awareness skills
▶ Increasing speed and accuracy of decoding/word attack skills
▶ Increasing speed of sight word identification
▶ Increasing speed of word retrieval, semantics, and vocabulary
▶ Increasing speed and fluency of connected reading
    Repeat reading
    Improving attention to details of the text
        Orthography
        Morphology
        Serial order of words
        Self-monitoring of meaning
        Prosody
        Syntactic structure and punctuation

In this book, I focus on activities in the last area—increasing speed and fluency of connected reading.

Why rate is important

Breznitz and Share (1992) have performed multiple studies in which the reading rate was manipulated. The studies "consistently supported the hypothesis that accelerated reading rate increased the level of comprehension and reduced decoding errors." Breznitz and Share conclude that these gains may be due at least in part to:

▶ Lower distractibility
▶ How the words sound when read more quickly, matching more closely the stored pronunciations

However, this 1992 study concluded that the improvements in comprehension that resulted from accelerated reading were "primarily attributable to changes in short-term memory processing."

Relationship of reading rate and short-term memory

Breznitz (1997) later tested this hypothesis among children with dyslexia. He found that "reading acceleration significantly enhances reading performance in specifically disabled readers. Dyslexic children can read faster than they normally do, and by doing so, increase decoding accuracy and comprehension." However, he found that readers with dyslexia may use short-term memory resources differently from novice readers (those novice readers which were reported in the 1992 study). One of those differences was that individuals with dyslexia were much more dependent on context. Breznitz concluded that "For dyslexic children, the effects of reading acceleration may enhance processing operations, whereas for normal readers acceleration may increase capacity."

Short-term memory and working memory are assumed to play an important role in reading. When a student has limitations in short-term memory, there is likely to be an impact on reading. Reading requires that the word or phrase being decoded be retained in this temporary storage while a student decodes it into a meaningful part of the text (Perfetti & Lesgold, 1977). Perhaps the processing operation that Breznitz refers to is the use of working memory for decoding.

Other explanations have been proposed for improved comprehension with increased reading rate. Based on Swanson's description of the relationship between short-term memory and working memory (1994), one interpretation is that fast-paced reading may improve reading effectiveness because it facilitates the interaction between short-term and long-term memory storage functions. That would allow better integration between top-down and bottom-up processing.

Individuals use a variety of strategies to minimize the limitations of short-term memory (e.g., the information can be retained typically about 30 seconds, only a limited amount of information can be held in working memory). They do this by organizing the information into chunks, rehearsing information, and parsing (Caplan, 1972; Jarvella, 1971; Kimball, 1973; Miller, 1956). Other researchers (Dempster, 1981; Torgesen & Houck, 1980) have found that increasing the stimulus presentation rate helps to overcome the limitations of short-term memory.

Connectionist theory and reading rate

Another explanation for why fast-paced reading helps individuals with dyslexia requires a description of a model of reading that is known as the *connectionist model* (Seidenberg, 1990). The connectionist model indicates that reading occurs when there is parallel activation of three subsystems:

1 Phonological
2 Orthographic
3 Semantic

The process starts when the brain receives an image of a printed letter string through visual processing. The brain recognizes this string by activation of appropriate codes in phonological and orthographic systems. These systems then activate the semantic system.

Perhaps working memory is the coordinating mechanism for information that arrives from each of those three subsystems. Breznitz (1997) hypothesizes that perhaps the fast-paced reading forces information to arrive in working memory at a faster rate, making it more likely that the corresponding information from the three subsystems will present at the same time.

We know that reading acceleration permits more efficient use of other cognitive abilities, such as attention. Breznitz hypothesizes that this faster-paced reading forces children with dyslexia to utilize other available cognitive resources more extensively.

Breznitz also hypothesizes that acceleration might shift the emphasis away from the slow phonological route to other, possibly compensating, routes for processing information during reading. Perhaps it forces the students to compensate for their phonological impairments by increasing their reliance on orthographic and contextual cues.

> **What happens when children read faster?**
>
> ▶ They make fewer pauses.
> ▶ They make shorter pauses.
> ▶ They vocalize at a faster rate.
> ▶ They speak in longer units.

Corrective feedback during reading

Most researchers agree that corrective feedback must be given when a student makes an error when reading aloud. If not, the student retains the wrong information about the word just misread. Some might think that stopping to correct the student would be detrimental. Any negative reaction to providing feedback during oral reading generally is related to one of three concerns:

▶ Frequent interruptions may make the reader rely on the external monitor, and this might discourage self-monitoring.
▶ Emphasizing error word recognition might detract from an emphasis on meaning.
▶ Feedback might be disruptive and interfere with the reader's attention to the story and, therefore, impair comprehension.

One study by Pany et al. (1981) demonstrates that corrective feedback was not detrimental to reading comprehension. Another study of third graders with learning disabilities (Pany & McCoy, 1988) found that when corrective feedback was given after every oral reading error, children made significant improvements. The students were also able to retell more story units.

Results of corrective feedback
▶ Significantly fewer overall errors
▶ Significantly fewer meaning change errors
▶ Significantly fewer errors on lists of error words
▶ Significantly fewer errors on passage comprehension questions

Most times, corrective feedback is simply stating the correct word when the student reads it incorrectly. A more detailed cueing and correction system could be used.

Several studies suggest that the most effective method of correction when a student misses a word in reading is word drill (Jenkins & Larson, 1979). Word drill involves noting any errors the student makes when reading, and then drilling on those words in mass practice at the end of the reading session.

Jenkins et al. (1982) investigated what effect single word error correction had on comprehension. They compared two strategies: word supply and word drill. In word supply, the instructor states the correct word after the student has made an error. The student then repeats the word and continues reading. The word drill method incorporated the above, but then had the student drill by practicing the words printed on index cards. This study concluded that the drill correction, which affects word recognition, also helps to improve comprehension of text that contains the original error words. The authors point out, however, that these were not large changes in comprehension, and other more specific activities for improving comprehension should be utilized if that is the goal.

Repeat reading

Assisted repeat reading is a technique in which the child reads the same passage several times in an attempt to increase speed and accuracy. Corrections are given when errors are made. Echo reading (also called choral or paired reading) is a variation of repeat reading. Each technique is described in more detail in the Appendices for Chapter 5. For a complete list of the Appendices in Chapter 5 and their page numbers, see page 40.

Appendices in Chapter 5 explaining repeat reading
D General Instructions
E Echo/Choral/Paired Reading
F Sprint
G Sprint + Drill
H Sprint + Style
I Count Down Method

What reading level should the text be when using repeat reading and other activities to help a child work on reading fluency? Some argue that the text should be easy (Clay, 1993), but most successful approaches use instructional level text or even text at the frustration level with lots of support (Stahl et al., 1997). Mathes and Fuchs (1993) found no effect for text difficulty. At the Reading Center, we use materials that the student can read with good accuracy. Most studies indicate that the student should be 90–95% accurate on the first read-through of the passage. Some studies, however, use slightly different percentages in their categories: 97–100% independent; 90–96% instructional; <90% frustration (Rasinski, 2003). Young and Bowers (1995) found that poor readers declined in reading rate, accuracy, and fluency as the text became more difficult. Therefore, in order for the student to concentrate on improving rate and fluency, the passages need to be easy enough that the student is not worrying about decoding and accuracy.

Does repeat reading help the student transfer this fluency to other text? Meyer and Felton (1999) describe this as a complicated issue. It may be the number of shared words in the text and it may be shared content that influences the transfer fluency (Rashotte & Torgesen, 1985; Faulkner & Levy, 1994).

How to select reading passages

When selecting text for the student to read, consider that most reading programs describe text at three different levels according to how accurate the child can be:

▶ Independent reading level   95% to 100%
▶ Instructional level   90% to 94%
▶ Frustration/hard level   89% or below

For repeat reading and other activities to build fluency, select text in the independent level.

Kuhn and Stahl (2003) indicate that approaches that involve rereading of text seem to be effective, though it is not clear why. It could be that it simply increases the volume of children's reading. It may also allow children to read more difficult material than they might be able to read independently, or it may be that it provides a structured way to increase amounts of reading. Kuhn and Stahl also indicate that most studies using repeat reading were with students in second or third grade or with older students with reading problems presumed to be reading at the primary level. It is at these grade levels that studies show gains with repeat reading. This is in concert with Chall's theory of stages of development of reading (1996). The second stage is called *confirmation* and fluency of "ungluing from print." In this stage, readers confirm what they know to develop their fluency. They need to become automatic with their recognition.

We have used repeat reading with older students with some success. We find it most helpful with students who are inattentive to the text (e.g., those who skip words, insert words, show a lack of attention to orthography and morphology) rather than with the ploddingly slow reader.

Providing correction of errors during repeat reading seems to be important. The correction can simply be the instructor saying the word the student has missed as soon as the error occurs. It can also involve drill activities on those missed words in between each repeat reading.

Meyer and Felton (1999) indicate that answering the question of whether repeated reading improves comprehension is difficult. That is because many of the studies that have assessed this have used different methods for measuring comprehension. Many of the researchers hypothesize that the reading practice helps the poor readers to become more efficient. This, in turn, enables them to shift their processing resources to comprehension. O'Shea et al. (1985) found that there was a difference when the instructor directed the student to pay attention to fluency or comprehension. If the student was asked to pay attention to fluency, she showed improvement in fluency but not as much in comprehension. If the student was asked to pay attention to meaning, she improved her comprehension and was better able to retell the story. These authors suggest that a combination of cueing the student for both fluency and comprehension would be ideal.

Meyer and Felton (1999) provide an excellent review of repeated reading in an article entitled, "Repeated Reading to Enhance Fluency: Old Approaches and New Directions." They report that repeated reading is based on the information processing model. This is the model that suggests that fluent readers can decode text automatically and leave their attention free for comprehension.

Samuels (1979) was one of the first to describe the method of repeated reading. He listed three goals:

1 Increase reading speed
2 Transfer improvement in speed to other material
3 Improve comprehension with each successive rereading of the text

Repeat reading has been found to have an affect not only on rate and accuracy, but also on speech pauses and intonation (Dowhower, 1987). Herman (1985) found that these effects transferred to previously unread material. Interestingly, repeat reading does not seem to improve rapid recognition of isolated words—the area for which it was actually developed (Kuhn and Stahl 2003).

Several research studies with both normal and disabled readers indicate that the most improvement in reading rate occurs after three or four readings. No significant change takes place beyond that number of readings (O'Shea et al., 1985; Bowers, 1993).

Meyer and Felton also indicate that most researchers recommend spending about 15 minutes a day in repeat reading. This time may include not only the fluency training, but also activities for correction of errors and testing for outcomes.

Paired reading

Paired reading is a non-repeated, assisted-reading approach. Topping and Whitley (1987, 1990) found that paired reading can significantly improve the student's reading fluency and overall proficiency. In paired reading, a capable reader and the struggling reader read in unison. The struggling student indicates when she is ready to try reading alone. When this student makes an error, the capable reader provides the correct word. The pair then reads the sentence with that word in unison and continues reading.

Appendix E in Chapter 5 on page 145 explains echo (also called choral or paired) reading.

Parent involvement with paired reading

Rasinski (1995) describes how paired reading is used. Each night the parent reads a brief poem or passage to her child. This is followed by the parent and child reading the text together several times. Then the child reads the text to the parent. Rasinski found that children who engaged in this form of paired reading made significant gains (in as little as five weeks) over children who got tutoring without this paired reading support.

If there is a question as to whether silent reading will also improve the student's reading performance, a study by Wilkinson et al. (1988) showed that silent reading does not have a significant effect on posttest reading performance. In addition, the National Reading Panel's examination of data (2000) failed to provide conclusive evidence that silent reading practice improved reading achievement. However, Kuhn and Stahl (2003) report that Krashen (2001) criticized the methodology behind this finding because certain studies were not included that did demonstrate the amount of time spent reading was a good predictor of reading achievement.

Improving attention to the details of text

Many non-fluent readers do not attend carefully to the details of the text. When they read, they demonstrate:

▶ Inattention to orthography
▶ Inattention to morphology
▶ Inattention to serial order of words
▶ Inattention to self-monitoring of meaning
▶ Inattention to prosody
▶ Inattention or lack of awareness of syntactic structure, including inattention to punctuation

> **Inattention to orthography**
> Students who don't attend to orthography may misread small words in the text (e.g., *if* for *of*, *full* for *fall*). They need practice to improve their attention to the actual words on the page. Activities to help them understand the importance of each and every word are indicated.

Inattention to morphology

Students who do not attend to morphology often miss word endings (e.g. *talk* for *talks*, *slow* for *slowly*, *jumped* for *jumping*). These errors may not affect comprehension when reading an article in a magazine, but they could, for instance, cause the student to complete a math problem incorrectly or misunderstand a science lesson.

Inattention to serial order of words

Some students move words around in the sentence, insert words, and skip words. This can indicate inattention to orthography but also an inattention to the serial order of words.

Inattention to self-monitoring of meaning

Some poor readers stop and question when what they are reading does not make sense. Others continue to read and seemingly fail to realize that what they have just read does not make sense. If the student is not monitoring meaning, stop frequently and ask her to paraphrase what she has just read and answer questions about that sentence or group of sentences. You'll find more information about comprehension strategies in Chapter 3.

Inattention to prosody and syntactic structure

Many authors believe that the student's inability to grasp the underlying syntactic structure and rhythmic characteristics of written language is a cause of dysfluency. In particular, Schreiber (1980) suggested that if the reader can understand the underlying syntactic structure, then she can read more automatically. Activities to help the students recognize the importance of punctuation can highlight the need for careful attention to that aspect of syntactic structure.

> **Prosody includes suprasegmental features**
>
> ▶ Intonation
> ▶ Stress
> ▶ Duration (including pause and juncture)
> ▶ Rhythm
> ▶ Timing

Increase recognition of phrases

Meyer and Felton (1999) suggest that for students with lack of sensitivity to prosodic cues, work should include helping the student recognize phrases within sentences. They suggest using techniques such as:

▶ Parsing exercises (separating noun and predicate phrases)
▶ Modeling prosody (listening to a fluent reader who is using good phrasing)

Several researchers have found that when students are presented with text that is segmented by phrase units, they can understand this better than conventional text. It seems to be most effective for children who are slow but accurate readers (Cromer, 1970; O'Shea & Sindelar, 1983). Perhaps this segmenting provides cues to phrasal structure like oral language does (Schreiber, 1980, 1987).

Hook and Jones (2002) indicate that students who read word-for-word need help with phrasing. They suggest this could start with the alphabet, having the student say or read the alphabet three letters at a time: *abc, def, ghi,* etc. They also describe a chunking machine, a *tachistoscope,* which allows the student to see chunks of the text through a window cut in an index card. Hook and Jones suggest that the student read the same set of phrases until she can pull the card quickly over the phrases and answer comprehension questions. See pages 165-180 for activities using a chunking machine.

Hook and Jones also describe the use of slash marks to mark phrasal boundaries in short passages. You can pre-mark the boundaries or let the student help you decide where to mark them.

Example of slash marks in a passage

Amanda wasn't ready. / Even though her dad / had told her / he'd be back by six, / she was still / getting ready. / They were going / to the monster truck show. / She had better get busy!

Hook and Jones further describe another method called *scooping* to help the student with phrasing. When using scooping, the student uses a finger or pencil to mark the phrases with a scoop mark. Hook and Jones (2002) suggest a hierarchy for teaching scooping:

1 Begin with baseline reading of the passage without scooping.
2 Practice selected phrases with scooping.
3 Practice selected sentences with scooping.
4 Practice paragraphs with scooping of sentences and pauses between.
5 Read again with scooping.

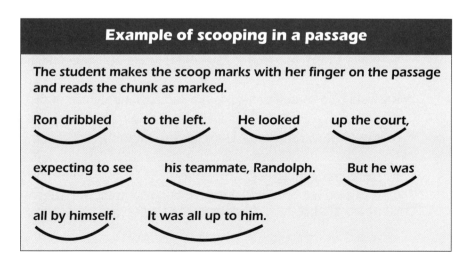

Example of scooping in a passage

The student makes the scoop marks with her finger on the passage and reads the chunk as marked.

Ron dribbled   to the left.   He looked   up the court,

expecting to see   his teammate, Randolph.   But he was

all by himself.   It was all up to him.

As students become more fluent readers, they recognize larger chunks of text at one time and move beyond the point of having to look word-by-word as they read.

Using poetry

Rasinski (2000) suggests that the use of poetry can help students attend to syntax and promote fluency. He thinks it is important that the repeat readings the child has to complete have a real reason. Otherwise, they may seem artificial and laborious. For instance, the student might have to read a passage several times in preparation of helping a younger student read it. (Note to the contrary: at the Reading Center, students do not find repeat reading laborious. We have found that most students enjoy competing against themselves, seeing if they can beat their last time.)

One study investigated using a readers' theater approach with second graders. In a ten-week implementation of this approach, small groups of second-grade students were introduced to, practiced, and performed a new script each week. The students made significant gains in reading rate and overall reading achievement (Martinez et al., 1999). Using this repeat reading approach, the students made an average rate gain of 17 WPM. Rasinski (1999) reported that 17 WPM is about the gain that can be expected in an entire year, so this change in ten weeks was significant.

If you can't use a full theater approach, have students read small dialogues to help with prosody. Drills for contrastive stress are also an excellent way to demonstrate to the students that intonation (in this case stress) can change the meaning and intent of the utterance. In contrastive stress drills, the student reads the same response several times as you ask questions.

Modeling appropriate expression

Rasinski (2000) also likes to model expressive reading for the students. After he reads the passage to the student with expression, he asks questions such as:

▶ What did the long pauses make you think of?
▶ Why did I read that part in a quiet voice?
▶ When I read this section fast, did it affect how you understood the story?

Rasinski also sometimes reads the students a sentence or passage from different perspectives, such as with an angry, sad, or surprised tone. Then he discusses the passage with the students. He states this helps the students by:

▶ Developing meta-cognitive understanding that the meaning of the passage is carried not only in the words, but also in the way the words are read
▶ Providing the model for students of what reading for meaning sounds like

Lack of prosodic cues in text

Perhaps part of the reason that some children have difficulty reading with expression is that the text has no markings to indicate what these prosodic features should be. More than 40 years ago, Fries (1963) pointed out that "In the graphic representation of language there are left out such language signals as intonation and stress and pause."

Schreiber (1980) hypothesized that the child's ability to compensate for the lack of prosodic cues may be what enables her to become a fluent reader. He proposes that the reason repcat reading works is that it gives the child the opportunity to recognize the importance of attending to prosodic cues. He indicates that it helps the student learn to rely on morphological and syntactic cues to parse the sentence into the appropriate phrases. The repeat reading, Schreiber states (1991), "affords readers the opportunity to perceive the syntactic organization of sentences."

Schreiber points out that there are many morphological, syntactic, and semantic cues within the sentence that help determine what the prosody should be. For example, the use of the word *those* in a sentence indicates that the noun is likely to be plural. It also gives information about the verb form which will appear. Schreiber states that the improvement in repeat readings is due to the child's ability to make better use of signals such as these in order to understand the prosodic cues. Although this hypothesis has not been fully substantiated in later studies, there is certainly some logic to the rationale that improving the student's understanding of and recognition of prosodic cues can only help to make her a more fluent reader.

In later work, Schreiber (1987) continued to discuss this hypothesis that fluency can only be obtained as the student masters recognizing and using prosodic cues. Gibson and Levin (1975) suggest that part of what makes the difference between good and poor readers is the reader's ability to segment written sentences into units such as phrases.

Conclusion

There are many other areas that must be addressed in order to help a student become a fluent reader (e.g., more efficient decoding, better word identification skills, attention to text). You must help the student put those skills together so that the fluency becomes apparent when the student reads connected text. Chapter 6 contains practice activities to address attention to text. Activities for other areas (e.g., word identification) can be found in *The Source for Reading Fluency* (Swigert, 2003).

The main focus of the activities in this book is to improve reading fluency; however, since the ultimate goal is for the student to understand what he has read, I have also included comprehension activities with the fluency passages in Chapter 5. Each story is followed by five questions. The first three questions require factual recall, while the last two items require the student to infer or draw a conclusion. The *Instructor's Guide to the Passages* (Appendix B on pages 135-142) also contains notes on some of the factual passages to assist with further discussion of these topic areas. There are many other strategies you can utilize to further develop comprehension. That information is briefly described in this chapter; however, this is not meant to be a comprehensive discussion of strategies to improve reading comprehension skills as that is outside the scope of this book. It is merely meant to provide you with ideas for other ways to use the reading passages to enhance comprehension.

Keep in mind that a student may appear to have a comprehension deficit when he really has a reading deficit (e.g., decoding, sight word identification, rate). That is, he can't read well enough to comprehend (see *The Source for Reading Fluency* [Swigert, 2003] for more information). Though it is always important to incorporate work on comprehension, you should have adequate diagnostic information about the student to determine if comprehension is really the issue.

What skills are required to comprehend a passage?

The skills required to understand a passage are varied and interdependent. The student must be able to **decode** or **recognize the words** in the passage. He must also be able to read the passage at an **adequate rate** (see Chapters 1 and 2). Additionally, the student should understand the **vocabulary** used in the passage. A student's reading vocabulary is closely mapped to his oral vocabulary. Students who seem to have difficulty with vocabulary comprehension may need a complete language assessment. Students also comprehend better when they have some **previous knowledge** or understanding of the topic; therefore, the knowledge the student brings to the reading passage plays a role in his comprehension of the passage. Sometimes students are able to answer comprehension questions based on this previous knowledge even when they haven't been very accurate in reading the passage. During our educational experience, I'm sure each of us has answered questions based on what we already knew and not what we studied (and forgot) from the lesson.

The student also has to have **adequate cognitive skills**, particularly working memory and short-term memory. If the student needs to improve his ability to remember and recall information that he read, then the passage should be covered up before presenting the questions. If instead, you want to help the student practice finding answers in the text, do not cover up the text. All in all, students have to attend to the story as they are reading. They also have to self-monitor for comprehension. Some students can read a passage quickly and fluently without paying a bit of attention to what they have just read. If the student is reading a fictional piece, knowledge of **story grammar** will be particularly useful. Different authors describe story grammar elements using slightly different terminology (Stein & Glenn, 1979; Duchan, 2001), but basically, each story has many of the following elements.

▶ Major and minor characters who are introduced in the story
▶ Setting in which the story takes place
▶ An initiating event or problem
▶ The main character's response to the event
▶ The plan devised by the character to address the problem
▶ Things that happen as a result of these actions
▶ A resolution to the problem

Knowledge of this common framework helps a student understand the passage as he reads.

The student also has to have **specific language abilities** that allow him to process and answer different kinds of questions or follow different kinds of questions. Depending on the kind of material the student is reading, he may have to:

▶ Compare and contrast information
▶ Answer a question that requires him to exclude information
▶ Utilize problem-solving skills
▶ Understand figurative language (metaphors, idioms, similes)
▶ "Read between the lines" by inferring information or drawing a conclusion
▶ Provide a synopsis of the information (summarizing)

Additional comprehension activities to use with the passages

In addition to using the questions provided with the passages in Chapter 5, you may also consider using the following strategies to give your students additional work on comprehension. Some of these may be more appropriate depending on the age of the students. Select activities based on your students' skills and on the goals you have for their comprehension.

Summarizing
Ask the student to summarize the passage. Summarization requires that the student has understood the gist of the passage. The student should not simply retell the story, but provide a synopsis.

Telling the main idea
Closely related to summarization is the ability to tell the main idea of the story. This is basically summarizing in one sentence.

Recalling details/facts
Each passage in Chapter 5 has three questions that require factual recall. You can come up with many other factual recall questions.

Building vocabulary
Identify any words in the passage that the student does not understand. Discuss the meaning of the word and help the student use it in other contexts. You could have

the student look up the meaning in the dictionary, or use a tool such as the *Franklin® Children's Talking Dictionary & Spell Corrector* (Model KID-1240CH) (www.franklin.com) or the *WizCom Readingpen®II* (www.wizcomtech.com).

Making predictions
Have the student stop reading in the middle of the passage and ask him to predict what might happen next. In the sequential stories (available for Levels A–C, grades 1–3), you can ask the student to make predictions between some of the passages concerning what might happen in the next passage.

Answering negative questions
Ask the student questions that require him to exclude options when selecting the correct answer. For example:

Which one is not _____?   Which one doesn't _____?
Why wouldn't _____?   What could have been done instead of _____?
Why shouldn't _____?

Learning to ask questions
Some students don't know how to ask a question to clarify information. They may simply state, "I don't get it," or even worse, they may not express their lack of understanding at all. Teach the student to ask specific questions.

Generating questions
Have the student generate questions about the passage for you to answer. At first students may ask simple questions that require only factual recall (e.g., What was the dog's name?), but with modeling and assistance, they should begin to generate more thoughtful questions (e.g., What if _____?, Why doesn't _____?, How _____?). A method called *Reciprocal Teaching* (Palinscar & Brown, 1984) includes a good description of question generation as a strategy as well as other strategies, such as summarizing/main idea, clarification, prediction, and question generation.

Pre-reading the questions
If you want to teach the student good study strategies, have him read the questions first to see what information is going to be important for him to attend to.

Visualizing
Some students benefit from learning to visualize the information they are reading to assist with comprehension and recall. One well-organized approach to teaching visualization is *Visualizing and Verbalizing* by Lindamood-Bell (1991).

Conclusion

Incorporating comprehension activities with fluency activities is important. It serves to remind the student that the ultimate goal is for him to understand what he has read.

The Problem with Readability Formulae

Readability analysis attempts to show how difficult a text is to read. These analyses provide a score or level of some type. I have provided information concerning the "level" of each of the passages, stories, poems, etc. in this book. However, before you choose a passage for a particular student based on the level information, you must be aware of the inherent flaws in any of the current systems used to provide such a grade level. You must also remember that what is ultimately important is that the passage must be appropriate for that particular student, regardless of her grade level and the indicated grade level on the passage.

Grading and leveling measures

Hiebert (2002) notes that the textbook industry tends to be a driving force in reading instruction in the United States. During most of the twentieth century, readability formulae heavily influenced the evaluation and creation of texts. Many different formulae were used. Since readability formulae were first developed in the 1920s (Lively & Pressey, 1923), they established the difficulty level of text on the basis of syntactic and semantic complexity. Syntactic complexity is typically determined by the number of words per sentence, whereas semantic complexity is typically measured by either word familiarity as compared to a particular list of words or by word difficulty as measured by the number of syllables per word. Words with three or more syllables are generally considered "hard" words.

What are some of the systems?

Two measures need to be described together—Flesch Reading Ease and Flesch-Kincaid Grade Level. These tests are designed to indicate how hard a passage is for a reader to understand. Although they reportedly use the same measures, just on a different scale, the results of the two tests don't always correlate. They're both based on the average number of syllables per word and words per sentence (Gunning, 2003; wikipedia, n.d.).

There are inherent flaws in these (and other) systems. We will summarize those flaws here in order to help you understand the need to place a limited value on a grade level when selecting passages to practice reading fluency with students.

Flesch Reading Ease
This formula scores passages on a scale of 0 to 100. The higher the score, the easier the material is to read. The lower numbers indicate that a passage is hard to read. This formula works on reading materials from fifth grade to college graduate, although it is usually used with adult material. The score is affected significantly more by long words in the passage than the Flesch-Kincaid Grade Level test described below.

scores of 90 – 100	understandable by an average fifth grader
scores of 60 – 70	understandable by eighth- and ninth-grade students
scores of 0 – 30	understandable by college graduates

For example, the average Reading Ease score for comic strips is 92, *The Readers Digest* has an average score of 65, *The Wall Street Journal* has an average score of 43, and *The Harvard Law Review* has an average score of 32. Standard insurance policies have an alarming average score of 10.

Flesch-Kincaid Grade Level
This formula translates the 0 to 100 score to a U.S. grade level. These grade levels are easier for teachers, parents, and others to use when judging the readability of different books. For example, a passage with the score of 4.5 indicates that a student in the fifth month of the fourth grade should understand the text. The Grade Level formula yields an index with a range from 1.0 (first-grade level) to 50 (totally unreadable). A high readability index (over twelfth grade) does not mean the writing is appropriate for college-educated readers; rather, it indicates that the writing is complex and difficult to read.

This formula is most reliable when used with upper elementary and secondary materials. The lengths of the sentences in the passage have an influence on the Flesch-Kincaid Grade Level. A passage with a higher percentage of longer sentences will yield a higher grade level. Renaissance Learning (2002) noted that the Flesch-Kincaid (and other formulae relying on syllables) underestimates the difficulty of nonfiction books. Gunning (2003) hypothesizes that this is because nonfiction books use specialized vocabulary that is not fully accounted for when just considering the number of syllables in the word.

The Flesch Reading Ease and the Flesch-Kincaid Grade Level measures are available in Microsoft® Word. I analyzed the passages in this book using Microsoft® Office Word 2003 SP2. Some other versions of Word use a different formula. The fact that the formula keeps changing in different versions underscores the lack of consensus in how to calculate readability scores and serves as a reminder that ultimately you must choose a text that is easy for the student to read, regardless of the readability score. If you're interested in using these measures to determine a reading ease or grade level for a particular passage, follow these steps to activate the readability statistics in Microsoft® Word:

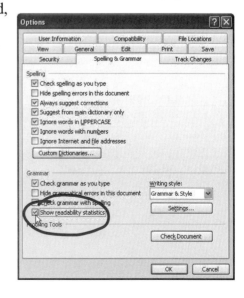

1 Click on the **Tools** menu.
2 Click **Options**.
3 Click the **Spelling & Grammar** tab.
4 Select the **Show readability statistics** check box.
5 Click **OK**.

After typing in a passage, you can display the readability statistics by highlighting the text and then selecting one of these options:

1 Click on the **Tools** menu, and then click on **Spelling & Grammar**.

2 Hit **F7**.

3 On the **Standard toolbar**, click **Spelling & Grammar**.

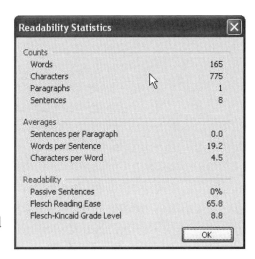

When Microsoft® Word finishes running a spelling and grammar check, a message box will appear asking you if you want to check the remainder of the document. When you select **no**, a box appears revealing the readability statistics. (Note: For unexplained reasons, Microsoft's version of the Flesch-Kincaid does not score above grade 12.)

Gunning-Fog

Other measures exist that provide a grade or a level. The Gunning-Fog method uses a formula based on the average number of words per sentence and the percentage of words with three or more syllables in a passage. The Fog method determines the readability level of materials between fourth grade and college. This formula, considered one of the easier methods for calculating readability, is based on a short sample of 100 words and does not require counting all syllables or applying many rules. It yields indices from six to 17, roughly equivalent to those grade levels (Gunning, 1952). The "ideal" Fog index level is seven or eight. A level above 12 indicates the writing sample is too hard for most people to read (Web Accessibility Technical Services, n.d.). This formula is often used in business publications.

Dale-Chall Formula

The Dale-Chall Formula (Intervention Central, n.d.) uses its own list of 3000 "familiar" words developed initially in 1948 and revised in 1983 (Dale-Chall List of Words, n.d.). These are words that 80% of fourth-grade children know (Weitzel, 2003). Chall considered these elemental words, such as words about home, family, food, etc. Words that the students learned primarily as a result of formal schooling do not appear on the list (Chall & Dale, 1995). In addition to considering the word list, Dale-Chall factors in the total number of words and sentences. It is designed for use in assessing upper elementary and secondary level materials.

Powers-Sumner-Kearl Formula

This formula is often used to assess materials for primary grades. It rarely produces a score above the seventh-grade level, thus exhibiting a ceiling effect. The formula takes into consideration the number of words, syllables, and sentences in a sample.

SMOG Formula

The SMOG Formula (McLaughlin, 1969) is relatively easy to use. It considers the number of words per sentence and the number of words over three syllables. Using a conversion number, the formula yields a grade level of four through 18. Most formulae predict 75 to 85% comprehension; however, the SMOG focuses on 100% comprehension. That means the SMOG formula will usually yield a higher grade level than most other formulae.

Fry Graph

The Fry Graph (Fry, 1968) displays its results as a dot on a graph. It uses the average number of sentences per 100 words and the average number of syllables per the same passage. It can be used on material from elementary school through college, though the extension through college was done by extrapolation (Fry, 1977). Fry acknowledges the lack of "pinpoint reliability" in his and other formulae. He indicates that Spache can identify a book within .6 of a year, and then only 50% of the time (Fry, 1968).

Spache Formula

The Spache Formula (Spache, 1981) uses a different approach. It is vocabulary-based and places weight on words not present in the formula's own word list. The formula works best for materials in primary through fourth grade. Because the results are based on the formula's own vocabulary list, two of the drawbacks to the Spache are:

1 The program is unable to recognize names.
2 The vocabulary is outdated (1981).

All of the formulae discussed thus far are available in a software program called *Readability Calculations* (Micro Power & Light Co., 2000). There are newer versions of the software, but the formulae haven't changed. This software also has a program called *Vocabulary Assessor*. This program will identify all of the words in a document and indicate how many times each one occurs in the passage. If you want the program to identify only words that might be hard for a certain group of readers, you have to supply a vocabulary list of words with which that group of readers is already assumed to be familiar. These vocabulary lists might be self-created or related to subject mastery. The program suggests that they might be available from the state education agency, but we were unsuccessful in locating any vocabulary lists at state or federal education agencies.

ATOS (Advantage-TASA Open Standard)

ATOS (Gunning, 2003) is a new computerized formula that uses the number of words per sentence, the number of characters per word, and the average grade level of the words. It analyzes the entire text to provide a grade level equivalent. To determine grade levels of words, Renaissance Learning, which produces *Accelerated Reader*, used *The Educator's Word Frequency Guide* (Zeno et al., 1995) and a list of words the company compiled.

Even with this new system, the company cautions that content needs to be considered. An author might be writing about a topic well beyond the abilities of, for instance, a fourth grader. But if the author uses short sentences and common language, the text might be rated for fourth grade.

Variability among these formulae

To demonstrate how different these formulae can be, the following passage was "graded" with some of the programs we have described. The results are shown in Table 1.

Randy looked longingly out the window as the snow continued to fall. He couldn't believe his bad luck! A day off of school because of snow, and he was stuck in bed with the flu. It hurt to lift his head from the pillow. His throat felt like it was made of razor blades. His eyes felt like they were on fire. Of all the days to be sick, he had to pick one when all his friends were outside sledding and having snowball fights.

Table 1	
Flesch Reading Ease	94.99
Flesch-Kincaid Grade Level	3.0
Gunning-Fog	5.3
Dale-Chall	4.8
Powers-Sumner-Kearl	4.1
SMOG	5.9
Spache	3.0

Additional systems

The Lexile Framework®

The most recent readability formula is the Lexile scale. Though its developers (Smith et al., 1989) claim that it is not a readability formula, Hiebert (2002) points out that Lexiles are computed using the same measures employed to compute readability—semantic and syntactic difficulty.

There are six ranges of Lexiles to cover the elementary grades as well as Lexiles to measure text through the college level (MetaMetrics, 2000). The elementary levels are described on the next page.

First Grade	200L to 370L
Second Grade	340L to 500L
Third Grade	480L to 670L
Fourth Grade	620L to 820L
Fifth Grade	770L to 910L
Sixth Grade	870L to 1000L

Hiebert (2002) criticizes the Lexile scale and illustrates this by reporting that *Harry Potter and the Goblet of Fire* (Rowling, 2000) has a Lexile of 880 while *The Firm* (Grisham, 1990) has a Lexile of 680. Heibert indicates that this points out the ambiguity of data on a scale from 200 to 1600—a scale which she describes as "dissociated from its semantic and syntactic criteria." There is no evidence provided about what word lists the authors used to develop the Lexiles.

Critical Word Factor
Hiebert (Hiebert, 2001a, 2001b; Hiebert & Fisher, 2002, 2003; Hiebert et al., 1995) has proposed a different method for measuring text difficulty. It was originally called the Complex Word Factor, but it is now known as the Critical Word Factor (CWF). This is an index of the word recognition demands of texts. The CWF is a function of the number of new, unique words per 100 running words of text that fall outside a designated group of high-frequency and phonetically decodable words. Hiebert's data indicates that the CWF is distinct from other commonly used readability formulae and Lexile ratings.

Text Leveling
Text leveling assigns texts as benchmarks for a certain grade level by experts in children's literature or in the processes of reading. Some states and some textbook publishers use experts to select the literature for a specific grade. The term "text leveling," however, comes from Reading Recovery (Peterson, 1991; Fountas & Pinnell, 1999, 2001). These levels are differentiated along four dimensions:

1 book and print features
2 content, themes, and ideas
3 text structure
4 language and literary elements

This system assigns books to levels A through R and cross-references these to grade levels K through 4. Reading Recovery has applied this system to categorize several thousand paperback books for children in grades K through 3, with word counts for most books. Hiebert (2002) found that these levels could not be applied reliably.

Shortcomings of methods

Hiebert (2002) indicates that when word recognition demands of textbooks are applied to books that have been assigned a level using one of the methods described in this chapter, there was little consistency within a set of books or across the different sets. She summarizes that text leveling doesn't provide sufficient information that would allow a group of experts to assign levels to texts. She also indicates that Lexiles don't inform teachers about the critical processes that readers are lacking. She challenges that substantial research needs to continue in this area.

Gunning (2003) also reviewed major readability formulae and leveling systems. He noted that readability formulae are restricted to the use of objective factors (e.g., number of syllables in a word) and that leveling systems rely too heavily on subjective judgment. He believes that both objective and subjective factors should be used when estimating readability levels.

Other considerations when choosing material

We have mentioned many factors for you to consider when choosing reading material for your students, including vocabulary, sentence length, word length, book and print features, etc. However, you must also consider the interests of the student. If you're working with a reluctant reader, the most important factor may be finding material about a topic that interests that student.

Since some students will prefer to read fiction while others will be more interested in fact-based content, you may wonder if one type of text works better than another in improving rate. Hiebert (2005) compared two groups of second graders who participated in Fluency-Oriented Reading Instruction (FORI). One group used literature in their repeat reading while the second group used content from science and social studies texts that contained few rare, multisyllabic, single-appearing words. The students who read the content material made greater gains in reading rate than the students who read literature.

What have some well-recognized programs used?

An online reading program called Reading A-Z (www.readinga-z.com) describes the criteria and book attributes it used to assign levels for its books. The criteria were based on analysis of published books that had been leveled using Fountas and Pinnell and Reading Recovery, along with other factors known to affect text difficulty. Reading A-Z indicates that they used objective criteria (e.g., total word count, high-frequency word count, sentence length) and subjective factors (e.g., picture support, concept difficulty, sentence complexity) that trained leveling specialists analyzed.

The Dynamic Indicators of Basic Early Literacy Skills (DIBELS) (www.dibels.uoregon.edu/) are a set of standardized, individually-administered measures of early literacy development. The measures were developed upon the essential early literacy domains discussed in reports from both the National Reading Panel (2000) and the National Research Council (1998) in order to assess student development of phonological awareness, alphabetic understanding, and automaticity and fluency with the code.

The DIBELS Oral Reading Fluency (DORF™) passages were generated to be used in benchmarking. After editing the passages for appropriate content and grammar, the developers of the passages used a complex process to determine their levels. Using the *Readability Calculations* software, they estimated the readability of all the passages. All readability estimates were computed, including Dale-Chall, Flesch Reading Ease, Flesch Grade Level, Fry Graph, FOG, Powers-Sumner-Kearl, SMOG, FORCAST, and Spache. It came as no surprise that the readabilities varied substantially and dramatically across the different readability formulae. Developers then used the Spache readability to revise and refine the passages to keep the Spache readability in a target range for each grade. They selected the Spache Formula because a second-grade analysis of the relation between readability formulas and empirical patterns of children's reading found the most support for the Spache Formula (Good et al., 2003).

Method used to grade passages in this book

Fully recognizing the shortcomings of any of the methodology used to determine a passage's readability, I made the following decisions when writing the passages for this book:

▶ I used the Spache Formula to determine the readability of the passages for grades 1 through 4 (Levels A through D). It didn't seem logical to use a method that didn't take vocabulary into account. Even if the vocabulary reference list is outdated, it shouldn't affect these passages as it would a textbook since I purposely avoided writing about "current" topics, such as computers, digital audio players, and cell phones.

▶ I used the Flesch-Kincaid Grade Level formula (from Microsoft® Office Word 2003 SP2) to analyze the passages for grades 5 through 8 (Levels E through H).

▶ I also used the Dale-Chall formula on the fifth-grade passages (Level E) to yield information about vocabulary words that might be difficult for the student. I noted any words in the passage that are not on the Dale-Chall list, which includes words that should be familiar to 80% of fourth graders (see Appendix B in Chapter 5, *Instructor's Guide to the Passages*, on pages 135-142). I didn't apply this formula to any of the other grade levels, but you could perform this analysis if you thought it would provide any useful information.

Choosing content for passages in this book

The passages for grades 1 through 3 (Levels A through C) are about fictional characters. This is true of both the sequential and the non-sequential passages. We did this for two reasons—to avoid difficult names of real characters and to maintain the student's interest. The passages for grades 4 through 8 (Levels D through H) are fact-based. This is because there has been some theoretical evidence suggesting the benefits of selecting informational text (Hiebert, 2005; Beck et al., 1984; Bruce, 1984). Content materials tend to repeat vocabulary words, thus exposing the student to new vocabulary multiple times. As noted above (Heibert, 2005), reading informational text may also increase reading rate more than reading literature.

Use the grade levels only as a guide

Most research concerning repeat reading as a technique to improve fluency indicates that the reading material should be something the student can decode automatically so that her attention is freed for comprehension. When selecting passages to use for repeat reading (or other practice materials for increasing attention to the text), select a passage that is at the independent or instructional level for that student. For students with very little confidence in their reading skills, you might use the independent level. The student will be more successful with that passage and gain confidence.

Reading Levels

Most reading programs describe text at three different levels according to how accurate the child can be:

▶ Independent reading level — 95% to 100%
▶ Instructional level — 90% to 94%
▶ Frustration/hard level — 89% or below

Conclusion

Understanding the limitations to any readability formulae, text leveling, or Lexile system is important when working with students with reading disorders. It explains seemingly illogical skill variations demonstrated by students. A student might read one passage or book at his grade level well—smoothly and accurately—yet struggle with another passage supposedly at the same level. Knowledge of these inherent weaknesses also makes you more aware of the care needed when selecting material for students to read.

This chapter contains graded passages for repeat reading for grades 1 through 8. Following each passage are five questions to improve comprehension—the first three ask the student to recall factual information that can easily be found in the passage, and the last two require the student to make an inference or draw a conclusion.

This chapter also includes several appendices related to using the reading passages (see below for a complete list). These appendices contain important information that you need to know before using the passages with students. You'll find general notes on using the passages (Appendix A), an instructor's guide that will help you select appropriate passages (Appendix B), and a form for tracking passages read (Appendix C).

Before using the passages for repeat or paired reading, read Chapter 4, beginning on page 31, for information on the methods I used to grade the passages. This chapter also contains information that will explain variances in your student's performance. You'll also need to read the appendices that explain how to complete repeat reading (Appendices D-I) and familiarize yourself with the charts and graphs that will help you to track the student's progress (Appendices K-P). Appendix J is a **No Guessing** sign that you'll find useful when working with students who don't attend well to the text and tend to guess rather than decode. You'll also need to familiarize yourself with how to compute words correct per minute (Appendix Q) and normative data against which to compare this rate (Appendices R and S).

List of Appendices for Chapter 5

1 Mac and Bell Dig a Hole

● ●

Mac and Bell live in a big house with a big yard. There is a big fence all the way around the yard. There is[25] a dog in the next yard named Sam. Mac and Bell want to play with Sam. Mac and Bell can't jump over the fence. They[50] decide to go under the fence. Mac and Bell start to dig. They dig and dig all day long. Finally the hole is big enough,[75] and they go under! Mac and Bell play with Sam. They chase Sam's ball. They jump in Sam's pond. They even roll in Sam's grass.[100]

    1. Where do Mac and Bell live?
    2. Who lives next door to Mac and Bell?
    3. How do Mac and Bell get out of the yard?
    4. What are Mac and Bell?
    5. Why can't Mac and Bell jump over the fence?

2 Mac Gets Stuck

● ●

Mac and Bell have been playing with Sam. Sam is the dog next door. Sam's owner has taken Sam inside. It is time for Sam[25] to eat his dinner. Mac and Bell are very hungry too. They want to go home and eat their dinner. They run back to the[50] hole they dug. Mac starts into the hole first. Something is wrong. Mac gets his head through the hole. Mac's body is stuck. Bell pushes[75] and pushes. Mac won't go through. Then Bell pulls and pulls, Mac can't come back. Mac is stuck tight.[94]

    1. Why did Sam go inside?
    2. Who took Sam inside?
    3. Why do Mac and Bell want to go home?
    4. Why does Bell push on Mac?
    5. Why do you think Mac got stuck?

Mac and Bell Are Rescued

Mac is stuck in the hole under the fence. He can't move at all.
Mac and Bell start to howl. Mac is scared. Mac and[25] Bell are hungry.
They want to go home. Then they hear their owner, Bobby, calling them.
"Mac and Bell, where are you?" Mac barks. Bell[50] barks. Bobby hears
them barking and runs to the fence. "How did you get stuck?" asks
Bobby. Bobby knows what to do. He runs and[75] gets a shovel. He
starts to dig. He digs until the hole is big enough for Mac to come
through. Then Bell comes through too.[100]

1. How does Mac feel when he is stuck?
2. What sound do the dogs make to call their owner?
3. What is their owner's name?
4. Why don't Mac and Bell answer Bobby when he asks how
   they got stuck?
5. How do you think Mac and Bell look after they come through
   the hole?

4 Bobby's New Pool

Bobby has a new pool. It has a big ladder. There is a big deck
around the pool. You can sit on the deck. You[25] can put your feet in the
water. You can stand on the deck. You can jump into the pool. Bobby
climbs the ladder. He walks[50] around the deck. Bobby jumps onto his
raft. He swims and swims. He waves to Mac and Bell. The dogs run
around and around the[75] pool on the ground. They bark at Bobby. They
want to be in the pool. They are hot.[93]

1. What is in Bobby's backyard?
2. How do you get into the pool?
3. What does Bobby jump onto in the pool?
4. Why is there a deck around the pool?
5. Why does the pool need a ladder?

5 Mac and Bell Learn to Climb

• •

Mac and Bell watched. Bobby stood on the deck. He jumped into the pool. Mac and Bell were very hot. Mac wanted to swim too.[25] He put his front feet on the first step. He jumped up on the step. Bell barked. Mac jumped on the next step. Bell jumped[50] up right behind Mac. They kept taking turns. Soon Mac and Bell were both on the deck of the pool.[70]

1. How did Bobby get into the pool?
2. Who watched Bobby jump into the pool?
3. Which dog started going up the steps first?
4. Why do you think Bell barked at Mac?
5. What do you think Bobby will do when he sees the dogs on the deck?

6 Mac and Bell Go for a Swim

• •

Mac and Bell are on the deck. Bobby is on his raft. It is very hot. Mac and Bell are panting. Bobby calls to the[25] dogs. Mac wags his tail. Bell wags his tail. They both stand up. They look at the water. It looks cold. They bark at Bobby.[50] "Woof," barks Bell. "Ruff," barks Mac. Then they both jump into the pool. They make a big splash. They paddle their feet as fast as[75] they can. They swim and swim. Bobby throws a ball. Bell and Mac race to get the ball. Bell gets the ball. Mac wants it.[100]

1. What do the dogs do when Bobby calls to them?
2. Where is Bobby?
3. What did Bobby throw for the dogs?
4. Why do you think Bell got to the ball first?
5. How could you tell the dogs were hot when they were on the deck?

7   Mac Takes Bell's Toy

● ●

Bell has a special toy. He likes it the best. It is an old green frog. It croaks when he bites it on the head.[25] Bell takes the toy frog with him when he goes outside. He sleeps with the frog. When he eats, he puts the frog by his[50] bowl. One day Bell is fast asleep. Mac sees the frog on the grass beside Bell. Mac sneaks over. He bites the frog on its[75] leg. It does not make a sound. Then Mac runs away as fast as he can.[91]

1. What is Bell's favorite toy?
2. What sound does the toy make?
3. What does Bell do with the toy when he goes outside?
4. Why does Mac bite the frog on the leg?
5. Why does Mac run away with the toy?

8   Mac Hides the Toy Frog

● ●

Mac runs fast. He has Bell's toy frog in his mouth. He looks for a good place to hide the frog. First he puts the[25] frog under a bush. He can still see the frog. Then he puts the frog under the steps. He can still see the frog. Then[50] he has an idea. He runs behind the doghouse. He starts to dig. He digs a deep hole. Then he drops the frog in the[75] hole. He covers it up with dirt. When he is done, no one can see the frog at all.[94]

1. How does Mac carry the toy?
2. Where is the first place he tries to hide the frog?
3. Where does he decide to hide the frog?
4. Why does Mac go behind the doghouse before he starts to dig?
5. How do you think Mac's paws look after he buries the frog?

9 Bell Misses His Toy

Bell wakes up from his nap. He looks for his toy frog. It is not in the grass where he left it. Did he leave[25] it in the doghouse? He runs and looks in the doghouse. The frog is not there. Did he leave it on the porch? He runs[50] and looks on the porch. The frog is not there. Bell is sad. Where is his frog? He asks Mac, "Have you seen my frog?"[75] Mac just smiles. Bell knows that Mac took the frog. Bell chases Mac and barks, "Give me back my frog."[95]

1. Where does Bell look for his toy frog?
2. How does Bell feel because his toy is lost?
3. Who does he think took his toy frog?
4. Why does Bell think Mac took the toy?
5. What do you think made Bell wake up?

10 Bobby Comes to the Rescue

Bobby hears Bell barking. He looks out the window and sees Bell chasing Mac. He runs outside and calls the dogs. "Come here, Mac and[25] Bell." Bell and Mac run to Bobby. "What is going on?" asks Bobby. Bell barks and barks and looks at Mac. "Where is your frog,[50] Bell?" asks Bobby. Bell barks again. Bobby shakes his finger at Mac. "Did you take Bell's toy?" he asks. Bobby walks around the yard looking[75] for the frog. Then he sees the dirt behind the doghouse. He kicks at the dirt with his foot until he sees the green frog[100] in the hole.[103]

1. What does Bobby see when he looks out the window?
2. What do Mac and Bell do when Bobby calls them?
3. Who does Bobby think took Bell's toy?
4. Why does Bobby shake his finger at Mac?
5. Why does Bobby kick the dirt?

1 The Cat and the Dog

∙∙

The cat sits on the bed. The dog looks up. He sees the cat on the bed. The cat sees the dog. The dog barks.[25] The cat jumps down. The cat runs. The dog runs too. The cat hides under the bed. The dog can't find the cat.[48]

1. Where does the cat sit?
2. What does the cat do when the dog barks?
3. Where does the cat hide?
4. Why does the dog bark at the cat?
5. Why does the cat hide from the dog?

2 Pete Cannot Sleep

∙∙

Pete goes to bed. He closes his eyes. He cannot sleep. He gets up. He reads a book. He plays with his cars. He pets[25] the dog. He jumps on the bed. Pete's dad comes in. Now Pete is back in bed. He will go to sleep now.[48]

1. What is the boy's name?
2. What does he do when he can't sleep?
3. What animal is in the room with him?
4. Why does Pete's dad come to his room?
5. What do you think Pete's dad said to him?

The Kite

Ken has a kite. It looks like a bird. It is red and blue. Ken can fly the kite. He can fly the kite at[25] the park. Ken and his dad fly the kite. Ken let go of the rope. He lost the kite. His dad was sad. The kite[50] is gone.[52]

1. What did the kite look like?
2. Who went with Ken to fly the kite?
3. What colors were the kite?
4. Why did they go to the park to fly the kite?
5. Why was Ken's dad sad?

Ruff Goes for a Ride

Ruff is brown and white. He has a long tail. Ruff loves to ride in the car. He rides in the backseat. The boy rides[25] with him. Ruff barks at trees. He barks at cars. He barks at houses. The boy tells Ruff to stop barking. Ruff sits down. He[50] does not bark.[53]

1. What color is Ruff?
2. What does Ruff like to do?
3. Who rides with Ruff?
4. What is Ruff?
5. Why does the boy tell Ruff to stop barking?

5 The Hot Day

It is a hot day. Pat is hot. He wants to swim. The pool looks good. The pool looks cool. Pat feels the water. It[25] is cold. It is deep. Pat finds his mom. His mom says he can swim. He gets in the pool. It feels good.[48]

1. What does Pat want to do?

2. How does the water feel?

3. Who does Pat go and find?

4. What does Pat ask his mom?

5. What time of year is it?

6 Jan Makes Up a Game

Jan plays with Ron. Jan has a ball. Ron has a rock. Jan puts the rock on the ball. The ball rolls. The rock falls[25] by Ron. Ron wins the game. Then Ron puts the rock on the ball. The ball rolls. The rock falls by Ron. Ron wins. Now[50] Jan is mad.[53]

1. Who is Jan's friend?

2. What does Jan have?

3. What does her friend have?

4. How do you win this game?

5. Why is Jan mad at the end of the story?

7 The Lost Hat

Jill has a hat. It is blue and white. She loves the hat. Her grandmother gave her the hat. Jill can't find her hat. She[25] looks on her bed. She looks on the floor. She looks in the van. She is so sad. Jill sees Sam. He has her hat[50] on his head.[53]

1. What color is Jill's hat?
2. Who gave Jill the hat?
3. Where does she look for the hat?
4. Why do you think Jill loves her hat?
5. What do you think Jill will say to Sam?

8 Ben Can Jump

Ben can jump. He can jump up on the step. He can jump down the step. He can jump off the bed. He can jump[25] on the rock. He can jump on one foot. He can jump on two feet. He does not hold on when he jumps. One time[50] when he jumped off the step, he fell. Ben hit his head. He cut his head. His mom gave him a hug. She told him[75] not to jump like that.[80]

1. How many feet does Ben use to jump?
2. What does Ben jump on or off of?
3. What did Ben hurt when he fell?
4. Why did Ben fall?
5. Why did Ben's mom give him a hug?

9   The New Bike

The boy got a new bike. It is red. His dad gave him the bike. The bike has a horn. The boy can ride the[25] bike in the park. He can ride the bike fast or slow. He likes to ride fast. His mom tells him to ride slowly. He[50] beeps the horn when he rides. His new bike is the best bike of all.[65]

1. What color is the bike?
2. Who gave the bike to the boy?
3. What does the bike have on it?
4. Why does his mom tell him to ride slowly?
5. Why does the bike have a horn?

10   Mike Can Draw

Mike likes to draw. He can draw with a pen. He can draw with a pencil. He draws on paper. Mike draws trees. He draws[25] bikes. He draws dogs and cats. One time he drew on the wall. His mom was mad. She made Mike wash the wall. Mike will[50] not draw on the wall again. He will draw on paper all the time.[64]

1. What does Mike like to do?
2. What does Mike draw?
3. How did Mike's mom feel when Mike drew on the wall?
4. Why did Mike's mom make him wash the wall?
5. Why won't Mike draw on the wall any more?

1 | Beth Helps Jed

Jed wanted to play soccer. He had played soccer in his backyard with his big sister, Beth, but he wanted to be on a team.[25] Beth showed him how to kick. She showed him how to pass the ball with his feet. She even showed him how to move the[50] ball down the field. Beth was on a team that had won all its games last year. Beth was a good soccer player. Sometimes Beth[75] played goalie and let Jed try to score. They had a goal with a net in their yard. They played soccer almost every day after[100] school.[101]

1. What is Jed's sister's name?
2. What do Jed and Beth have in their backyard?
3. When did Beth help Jed with soccer?
4. How do we know Beth's team is very good?
5. How do we know Beth is a helpful big sister?

2 | Jed Kicks Too Hard

One day after school, Beth was not home. Jed went to the yard by himself because he wanted to try kicking the ball. He stood[25] close to the goal and kicked. He missed the goal. He tried again and made it. Then Jed backed up a little bit. He kicked[50] again, but the ball didn't go as far as the net. The next time Jed kicked really hard. The ball went past the net and[75] into the yard next door. A really big, mean dog lived there. The dog, named Spike, was barking at Jed. Jed wanted his ball back,[100] but he did not like the dog.[107]

1. What did Jed want to practice this day after school?
2. Where did the ball go when Jed kicked it really hard?
3. What was in the yard next door?
4. Why was Jed practicing by himself?
5. Why do you think Jed doesn't like the dog next door?

3   Jed has an Idea

Jed has to get his ball back, but Spike is right by it. Jed has a dog too. Jed's dog likes to go for walks[25] on a leash. When they walk past the dog next door, Spike barks at Jed's dog. Jed gets his dog, Buster, and puts on his[50] leash. He walks Buster past the front of the yard next door. Spike runs to the fence in the front and barks at Buster. Jed[75] ties Buster to a tree and Spike keeps barking. Jed runs to the side yard and sneaks in the gate. He gets his ball and[100] comes back to get Buster.[105]

1. What is the name of Jed's dog?
2. What does the dog next door do when he sees Jed's dog?
3. Where does Jed tie Buster?
4. Why does Jed tie up Buster when he goes to the side yard?
5. Why does Jed put a leash on Buster when he walks him?

4   Buster Is Missing

When Jed comes back to the front yard, Buster is not there. His leash must have come untied! Jed looks up and down the street.[25] He doesn't see Buster anywhere. Jed yells for Buster. He whistles for Buster. Where could that dog be? Jed is very scared. He knows Buster[50] likes to run into the street. He doesn't want Buster to get hit by a car. Jed is just about to run home and tell[75] his mom when he sees Buster. Buster has crawled under the fence and is in the backyard with Spike![94]

1. What does Jed find when he comes back to the front yard?
2. How does he try to call Buster?
3. How does Jed feel when he can't find Buster?
4. How do you think Buster got loose from the tree?
5. What might happen to Buster if he runs into the street?

5 Buster and Spike

Buster and Spike are playing. Spike has Buster's leash in his mouth and is pulling on it. Buster is pulling back. It is like a[25] game of tug-of-war. Spike lets go of the leash and finds his ball. He drops it in front of Buster. Buster takes the ball and[50] runs around the yard. Spike runs after him barking. The dogs look like they are having a lot of fun. They are not barking at[75] each other. Maybe Spike barked at the back fence all the time because he wanted a friend. Maybe Spike is not a really mean dog[100] after all.[102]

1. When Jed looks through the fence, what does Spike have in his mouth?
2. What does Buster do when Spike drops the ball by him?
3. What does Spike do when Buster runs with the ball?
4. Why aren't the dogs barking at each other?
5. Why does Jed decide that Spike isn't a mean dog after all?

6 Game Night for Beth

Beth's team has a game tonight. Jed is going to the game with his mother and father. His dad doesn't get to go to all[25] the games. Sometimes he has to work too late. They are going to stop at Casper's and get something to eat before the game. Jed[50] will probably get a cheese sandwich and French fries. Beth always gets a burger and fries. After they eat, they will go to the field[75] that is near their school. Beth's coach wants the team on the field one hour before game time to warm up. Beth gets to start[100] tonight for the first time.[105]

1. Who is going to Beth's game?
2. Why doesn't Beth's dad get to go to all the games?
3. What will Beth eat at Casper's?
4. Why does Beth's dad get to go to this game?
5. How do you think Beth feels about getting to start the game?

7 Beth Scores

Beth's team is called the Rockets, and they are playing a team called the Legends. These two teams have never played each other before. The[25] Legends are one of the best teams around. Their best player is a girl named Becky, and she is guarding Beth. The game is almost[50] over and the score is nothing to nothing. Beth is running down the field when another girl on her team, Amanda, passes the ball to[75] Beth. Beth kicks it straight at the goal. The Legends' goalie jumps but cannot block it. Beth has scored! She and her teammates jump up[100] and down. Now they are winning![106]

1. What is the name of Beth's team?
2. Who is the best player on the other team?
3. What is the name of the other team?
4. After Beth scores a goal, what is the score of the game?
5. Who do you think wins the game?

8 The Celebration

The Legends are not able to score in the minutes left in the game. The Rockets have the victory. Beth is the hero of the[25] game. Her coach lifts Beth up on his shoulders. The other players on her team are cheering. Everyone watching the game is clapping and yelling.[50] Beth's mom and dad take the whole team to Cool's. Almost everyone gets a milkshake. Jed orders an ice-cream cone. The parents and coach talk[75] about the game. They also talk about the team the Rockets will play next. Everyone has a good time.[94]

1. What does Beth's coach do to her?
2. What are the people watching the game doing?
3. Where do Beth's parents take the team?
4. What kind of place is Cool's?
5. Why was Beth the hero?

9 Jed Joins a Team

Beth has helped Jed a lot with soccer. Jed can pass and kick the ball well. He can run faster without getting tired. Beth thinks[25] Jed is ready to play on a team. When Jed sees a sign-up sheet at school for a new soccer team, he signs up. The[50] new team will be called the Wizards. Jed's friends Marco and Dan sign up too. The first meeting of the team will be on Friday[75] after school. Players will get their uniforms and meet their coach. They will practice after school. Their games will be on the weekends.[98]

1. What does Jed do when he sees the sign-up sheet?
2. What is the new team called?
3. When is the first team meeting?
4. Why does Beth think Jed is ready to play on a team?
5. Why do you think the games will be on the weekends?

10 Jed's First Game

Jed and the Wizards have been practicing hard for weeks. Now they are ready for their first game. Jed's parents and his sister, Beth, are[25] there to watch him. Jed likes the uniforms his team wears. They are blue with yellow trim. The coach has a hard time deciding who[50] will start. Jed's friend Marco gets to start, but Jed has to wait for a turn to play. Jed does get to play a few[75] times in the game. He makes a few good passes. The other team wins, but Jed's coach tells the Wizards that he is proud of[100] them. They will practice the things they need to improve.[110]

1. Who came to watch Jed's first game?
2. What colors are on Jed's uniform?
3. What does Jed do well in the game?
4. Why did Marco get to start instead of Jed?
5. Why is the coach proud of the Wizards even though they lost?

1 Josh Finds a Bug

....

Josh sits in the grass. He digs in the dirt. He finds a bug. The bug is black. The bug has eight legs. The bug[25] has a yellow dot on its back. The bug is not big. The bug bites Josh. Josh drops the bug.[45]

1. Where does Josh sit?
2. What color is the bug?
3. How many legs does the bug have?
4. Why does the bug bite Josh?
5. Why does Josh drop the bug?

2 Muffy Climbs a Tree

....

Muffy gets out of the house. She runs fast to a big tree she sees in the yard. She climbs the tree. She is up[25] high and can see far away. She wants to come down, but she cannot get down. She cries and cries until a girl hears Muffy[50] and comes to the tree. The girl will help Muffy.[60]

1. What does Muffy see in the yard?
2. Where does Muffy go when she gets out of the house?
3. Who will help Muffy?
4. How do you think Muffy got out of the house?
5. How will the girl help Muffy?

3 Snake in the Grass

• •

Becky is outside without shoes running in the grass. She steps on something that moves away fast. Becky looks down and sees a snake. She[25] yells very loudly and points at the grass. Her sister Jane comes to see why Becky is yelling. Jane starts to yell too. The girls[50] run back into the house. Becky puts on her shoes before she goes back out.[65]

1. What does Becky step on?
2. Who comes when Becky starts yelling?
3. What does Becky do when she goes back into the house?
4. What do you think Becky said to Jane when she came outside?
5. Why does Becky put on her shoes?

4 Sam Bakes a Cake

• •

Sam wants to make a cake. He likes white cake. Mom will help. Sam gets the bowl. Sam gets the egg. Sam gets the milk.[25] Sam stirs and stirs. Sam licks the spoon. They bake the cake. It is too brown. Sam is so sad. The cake is no good.[50]

1. What does Sam want?
2. What kind of cake does Sam like?
3. What does Sam do with the spoon?
4. Why will Sam's mom help him?
5. Why did the cake come out too brown?

5 Steve and Mom Bake

Steve comes home from school one day. He looks very sad. His mother asks Steve why he is sad. He shows her the grade he[25] got on his spelling test. He had studied hard for the test. His mother knows what will make Steve feel better. She and Steve bake[50] some cupcakes for the family. Steve does feel better.[59]

1. How does Steve feel when he comes home from school?
2. What kind of test did Steve have at school?
3. What do Steve and his mom do together?
4. What kind of grade do you think Steve got on his spelling test?
5. Why did Steve's mom ask him to help her bake?

6 The Magic Jacket

Uncle Hal was Allen's favorite uncle. On Allen's birthday, Uncle Hal gave him a purple jacket. He told Allen it was a magic jacket. When[25] you put your hands in the pockets, you will find some coins. Allen put his hand in one of the pockets and found a dime![50] He reached into the other pocket and pulled out a penny. Maybe the jacket really was lucky![67]

1. Why did Uncle Hal give Allen a jacket?
2. What color was the jacket?
3. What did Allen find in the pockets?
4. Why do you think Uncle Hal is Allen's favorite uncle?
5. Do you think Allen will find a coin every time he reaches in the pocket? Why?

7 The New Coach

It was the first day of baseball practice. Jerry and Maria were on the same team this year. Last year their team won only two[25] games. They hoped their new team would be better than last year's team. They were happy to see that they had a new coach. Her[50] name was Coach Hernandez, and she had a daughter on the team.[62]

1. What sport do the children play?
2. How did their team do last year?
3. What is the new coach's name?
4. Why do they hope this is a better team than last year?
5. Why are they happy to have a new coach?

8 Drew's First Solo Flight

Drew lived with his mother and father in Maine. Drew's grandparents lived in New York. Drew was going to spend the summer with his grandparents.[25] His mother took him to the airport, but she was not going to fly with him. Drew's mother took him to the gate and watched[50] him get on the plane. As the plane took off, Drew felt sad and happy at the same time.[69]

1. Where does Drew live?
2. Where was he going for the summer?
3. How was Drew going to get there?
4. Why wasn't Drew's mother going with him?
5. Why did Drew feel sad and happy?

9   Disney World

• •

Kevin and Melissa were going to Disney World with their family!
Kevin and Melissa had earned this trip by getting good grades. When
the family[25] arrived at Disney World, they parked their car in a big lot.
Then they rode a little train to the boat. They rode the boat[50] across
the lake to the main gate. Their dad bought tickets for the whole family.
They planned to ride every ride in the park and[75] stay until it was dark.[80]

1. Where were Kevin and Melissa going on their trip?

2. Where did the family park their car?

3. How did they get across the lake?

4. How do you think Kevin and Melissa felt about their trip?

5. Why will they stay until it is dark?

10   The Shopping Trip

• •

Kirk's mother found him hiding in the basement. She told him
it was time to go shopping for new school clothes. Kirk slowly climbed
the[25] stairs. He followed his mom to the van. They went to the mall and
bought new jeans and three shirts. Kirk asked for a new[50] backpack.
His mother told him he didn't really need a new one. She did buy him
a new baseball cap.[70]

1. Where was Kirk hiding?

2. Where was Kirk's mom taking him?

3. What did Kirk ask for?

4. Why was Kirk hiding in the basement?

5. What time of year do you think it is?

The Walled City

⋯⋯⋯⋯⋯⋯⋯⋯⋯⋯⋯⋯⋯⋯⋯⋯⋯⋯⋯⋯⋯⋯

Lucas lived in Italy in 1570 in a city surrounded by earthen walls twenty feet tall. The walls were ten feet wide at the top,[25] and a pathway circled the city on the top of the walls. The walls were built to protect the city, called Vorino, from its enemies.[50] The city had four gates, one on each side of the city, which were each guarded at all times by four strong soldiers. The guards[75] patrolled inside the gate and on top of the wall. Lucas's father was the leader of the guards. Lucas sometimes went to work with his[100] father and talked with the other guards. He wanted to be a guard when he was old enough. You had to be fifteen years old[125] to join the guards. Lucas was only eleven.[133]

1. What was the name of the city where Lucas lived?
2. Why did the city have a wall around it?
3. How many soldiers guarded each gate?
4. Why did Lucas like to go to work with his father?
5. How many years does Lucas have to wait until he can be a guard?

2 Lucas and His Family

Lucas lived with his father and mother and his older sister, Carlotta, who was thirteen. She liked telling Lucas what to do and was especially[25] good at choosing times to boss Lucas around. She never did it when his mother and father were at home. Carlotta thought that because she[50] was older, she knew everything. Lucas thought that Carlotta was jealous of him because she couldn't do some of the things he could do. Girls[75] weren't permitted to leave the house after dark unless their fathers were with them. Lucas's father was often on guard duty at night. This meant[100] Carlotta was stuck at home most evenings. Girls weren't allowed to try out for the guard. Lucas thought that was what Carlotta secretly wished she[125] could do. Lucas sometimes saw Carlotta trying on their father's heavy helmet and his sandals.[140]

1. When does Carlotta tell Lucas what to do?
2. What can boys do that girls can't?
3. How old was Lucas's sister?
4. How many people lived at Lucas's house?
5. Why did Lucas think Carlotta wanted to be a guard?

3 | Lucas's Secret Missions

On the nights his father went to work, Lucas left the house too. His mother and sister were not aware that Lucas was gone. He[25] would wait until his mother had checked on him and believed him to be sleeping. Then he would quietly slip from his bed and put[50] on his shoes. He grabbed the lantern he kept hidden under his bed and quietly pulled back the curtain covering his window. He slipped outside[75] and lit the lantern. It was against the law to be out after dark without a lantern. Lucas's house was near the edge of the[100] city on the east side, so it only took him a few minutes to make his way to the wall. He avoided the gates because[125] he didn't want any of the guards to know he was out and tell his father![141]

1. Where did Lucas keep his lantern hidden?
2. What did Lucas's mother think he was doing when he was really outside?
3. How did Lucas get out of the house?
4. Why did Lucas wait until he was outside to light his lantern?
5. Why might it be against the law to be outside after dark without a lantern?

4 The Guards

The guards of the city of Vorino were chosen from the strongest young men in the town. When a boy turned fifteen, he could sign[25] up to try out for the guards. Tryouts were held each spring in the center of the city. The competition was fierce as most young[50] men wanted to join the guard. Most of the citizens of Vorino came to watch the competition. Each contestant was required to run around the[75] city on the top of the wall. The 10 fastest runners advanced to the other competitions. These included jousting and throwing a weapon that looked[100] like a long spear. The two young men who scored the most points in these final competitions were welcomed into the guard. For the first[125] year, they each served as an apprentice to a more experienced guard.[137]

1. How old did a boy have to be to try out for the guard?
2. Who came to watch the tryouts?
3. What was the first contest when trying out for the guard?
4. Why did a first year guard have to serve as an apprentice?
5. Why weren't tryouts held in the winter?

● ●

Lucas walked as quietly as he could, keeping close to the walls and in the shadows, trying not to kick any loose stones. Though he[25] knew he shouldn't, he found his way to the steps that led to the top of the wall. It could be dangerous to be on[50] top of the wall after dark because a scout from the enemy city of Tensa could be hiding on the other side of the wall.[75] Staying low to the ground, Lucas crept along until he was directly above the east gate. The guards, with their uniforms polished and gleaming, were[100] stationed below talking. Lucas put out his lantern, dropped to the ground, crawled to the edge until he was close enough to see, and peered[125] into the darkness. One guard was drawing a map in the dirt. It seemed to be a map of Tensa. Lucas wondered if they were[150] planning an attack. The two cities had not had a war in over three years. Lucas hoped that wasn't the plan.[171]

1. Which gate did Lucas go to first?
2. How did Lucas get to the top of the wall?
3. What is the name of the enemy city?
4. Why did Lucas put out his lantern?
5. Why did Lucas stay low to the ground as he moved around the wall?

Lucas Starts His Patrol

Lucas decided that he would circle the city, staying on the path on top of the wall. His plan was to stop at each gate[25] to see what the guards there were talking about. If a fight was planned, he wanted to be the first to know. He knew his[50] father wouldn't tell the family if the guards knew of such a plan. They were sworn to secrecy regarding plans for the safety of the[75] city. In the past, there had been spies from Tensa who had moved into Vorino and tried to obtain information from friends and families[100] of the guards. Lucas picked up his lantern but kept the light off. He ran as fast as he could to the south gate where his[125] father was stationed for the night. His father and one other guard were patrolling along the top of the wall, which they did once an[150] hour. They didn't seem worried at all about their enemies from Tensa. Lucas had to creep through the trees to keep from being seen.[174]

1. At which gate was Lucas's father stationed on this night?

2. What was Lucas's plan for patrolling the city this night?

3. What city had sent spies to Vorino in the past?

4. Why wouldn't Lucas's father tell the family if an attack were planned?

5. Why did the guards go to the top of the wall to patrol?

Lucas Circles the City

Lucas continued running, though his legs were growing tired. It took about fifteen minutes for him to reach the next gate on the west side[25] of the city. Here the guards were also relaxed, laughing quietly and drinking cool water from a flask. Lucas wondered why the guards at the[50] east gate seemed to be the only ones who were even talking about the enemy. Just as he was about to stand up and start[75] running toward the north gate, Lucas heard a noise. It came from the top of the wall and sounded like it was only ten feet[100] away. Lucas held his breath and listened. There it was again. It sounded like stones being crushed under someone's foot. The guards stationed below didn't[125] seem to hear it, though to Lucas it sounded as loud as a volcano erupting.[140]

1. What were the guards at the west gate doing when Lucas got there?

2. What made Lucas stop when he was ready to run?

3. What did the noise sound like to Lucas?

4. Why could Lucas hear the noise, but the guards didn't?

5. What do you think is making the noise?

· ·

Lucas peered into the darkness and saw a shape moving toward him. Someone was approaching from the opposite direction. A lantern hung from the person's[25] arm, but it was also extinguished. Lucas slid behind one of the tall trees that grew along the top of the wall and waited until[50] the person was less than three feet away. Then he saw the person clearly. It was Carlotta! She was out after dark without a lantern[75] or her father. She would be in big trouble if their father found out! Lucas whistled softly, a secret whistle he knew Carlotta would recognize.[100] She stopped in her tracks and swung around. Not wanting the guards below to hear, Carlotta and Lucas signaled to one another. They did not[125] speak until they were close enough to whisper. Lucas told Carlotta what he had seen the guards drawing at the east gate. Carlotta shocked Lucas[150] when she told him that she had just come from the north gate, and the guards there were talking about an attack planned for next[175] week.[176]

1. Who did Lucas see on the top of the wall?
2. Why would Carlotta be in trouble if her father saw her?
3. How did Lucas feel when Carlotta told him about the planned attack?
4. Why were Lucas and Carlotta whispering?
5. Why didn't Lucas call out Carlotta's name?

Lucas and Carlotta Spot a Problem

Lucas and Carlotta decided that they should try and get home in the quickest way possible. Just as they turned to go down the stairs,[25] Carlotta dropped her lantern. It rolled to the edge of the path near the outer limit of the wall. Lucas hurried over and bent down[50] to pick it up, peering over the edge of the wall. Lucas could hardly believe his eyes. Approaching from the forest were four scouts from[75] Tensa, carrying weapons and wearing full armor! Lucas whistled softly, and Carlotta crawled to the edge of the path and looked over the wall. She[100] gasped when she saw what Lucas had been watching. They had to warn the guards below. They needed to do it without the guards learning[125] that Lucas and Carlotta were out after dark.[133]

1. What made Lucas go to the edge of the wall?
2. What did Lucas see when he looked over the wall?
3. How did Lucas get Carlotta's attention?
4. Why did Lucas and Carlotta decide they should go home?
5. Why do they need to tell the guards what they saw?

Lucas and Carlotta quickly ran down the steps as quietly as they could. The guards were facing the other way, polishing their weapons. Luckily the[25] moon was behind the clouds and it was dark. Their plan might just work. Lucas climbed onto Carlotta's shoulders. He wrapped her long, black cloak[50] around his shoulders so it hung low and covered Carlotta to the waist. In the dark, the guards just might believe they were talking to[75] a tall man! Carlotta, with Lucas on her shoulders, ran toward the guards. Lucas shouted the warning that they had seen Tensa scouts on the[100] other side of the wall. The guards sent a runner to alert the soldiers in the guardhouse nearby, and they prepared to go through the[125] gate to capture the scouts. In the confusion, Lucas and Carlotta slipped quietly away and back to their house.[144]

1. What were the guards doing when Lucas and Carlotta got to the bottom of the stairs?
2. What did Lucas use to hide Carlotta's face?
3. Where did Lucas and Carlotta go after they warned the guards?
4. Why did Lucas need to sit on Carlotta's shoulders?
5. Why did the guards send for more soldiers?

1 Smoky Mountains

Harry and his family were going on a vacation, and he and his sisters were sitting in the back of the van. Harry was stuck[25] sitting between his sisters because the girls always fought if they sat next to each other. His dad told him they would soon be driving[50] through the Smoky Mountains. Harry thought that seemed like a strange name for mountains. When his dad cooked on the grill, the backyard sometimes got[75] smoky, and when he went to his grandpa's house and they burned leaves, the air got smoky. But smoky mountains? Just then Harry looked out[100] the front window of the van and saw the mountains ahead. It really did look like there was smoke all around them. It turns out[125] that Smoky was the perfect name for the mountains.[134]

1. Why weren't Harry's sisters allowed to sit next to each other in the car?
2. What kind of vehicle did Harry's family have?
3. What are the mountains called?
4. How many children are in Harry's family?
5. Why would the backyard get smoky when Harry's father cooked on the grill?

Paula was spending the whole summer with her grandmother in her big, old house in the country. Paula loved being with her grandmother during the[25] day because her grandmother had a horse and she taught Paula how to groom it. Paula could ride the horse every day if she wanted[50] to. The days were great, but it was the nights that Paula hated. The room Paula slept in was on the top floor of the[75] house, and there were windows on three sides of the room. There weren't any curtains on the windows, so the room was never really, really[100] dark. When Paula was in bed, she heard creepy noises and saw very strange shadows on the wall. The shadows moved, and sometimes they even[125] changed shapes. Paula didn't want to tell her grandmother that she was afraid of shadows because her grandmother would think Paula was a scaredy-cat.[149]

1. What did Paula like to do at her grandmother's house?
2. When did Paula stay with her grandmother?
3. Where was Paula's room at her grandmother's house?
4. Why do you think Paula spent the summer at her grandmother's house?
5. What do you think caused the shadows on the wall?

Juan was not looking forward to tomorrow. He and his family had moved to Smithville over the summer. Juan's mother had gotten a new job[25] there. Juan had made friends with the boy next door, Bob, but he hadn't met many other kids his age. Bob did not go to[50] the same school where Juan was going. Juan's mother said she would walk with him to school tomorrow, but Juan didn't want anyone to think[75] he was a baby. He made her promise she would not go into the classroom with him when they got there. There might be things[100] worse than being the new kid in class, but right now, Juan couldn't think of what that might be.[119]

1. Why didn't Juan want his mother to go to class with him?
2. Who was Juan's neighbor?
3. What was the name of Juan's new town?
4. Why was Juan not looking forward to tomorrow?
5. If Bob and Juan live next door, why don't they go to the same school?

4 The Birthday Party

Amanda went to the mailbox and brought the mail into the house. She did this almost every afternoon when she got home from school, but[25] today something was different. Today there was an envelope, pink with yellow and green candles around the edges, addressed to her! Amanda tore open the[50] envelope, pulled out the card, and saw the words "You Are Invited" printed across the front of it. Amanda's heart beat a little faster as[75] she opened the card to see who sent it. She couldn't believe her eyes! She was invited to a party for Mindy this Saturday. Mindy[100] was the most popular girl in the class. Amanda would have to ask her mother to take her shopping before Saturday.[121]

1. When did Amanda pick up the mail?

2. Why was Amanda surprised when she picked up the mail?

3. What was printed on the front of the card?

4. What kind of party was it going to be?

5. Why does Amanda need to go shopping?

5 The Lost Money

Where could it be? Nick checked his pockets for the second time. He was sure he had put the ten-dollar bill, money for the field[25] trip his class was taking today, in the front pocket of his jeans. They were all going to the Children's Museum, and then they were[50] going to have lunch at a restaurant. The permission slip was right there in his pocket, and he was sure his dad had given him[75] the money and the slip at the same time. If you didn't have your permission slip and your money, you had to stay at school.[100] Nick had been looking forward to this field trip. Nick was about to raise his hand to tell his teacher about his bad luck when[125] he looked down at the floor. Nick smiled and reached down to the floor.[139]

1. What had Nick lost?
2. Where was the class going on a field trip?
3. What two things did the students need in order to go on the trip?
4. Why did the students need money for the trip?
5. Why did Nick smile when he looked down at the floor?

6 Going Camping

Lucy's mother had a new boyfriend called Peewee. Lucy didn't think Peewee was his real name, but that's what everybody called him. Peewee wanted to[25] take Lucy and her mother on a camping trip. The trip would require them to bring along a tent and hike into the mountains. They[50] would have to sleep on the ground in sleeping bags. Peewee had a little stove they could use to cook their food. Lucy had never[75] been camping and didn't want to start now. She hated bugs and thought there must be lots of bugs and other creepy, crawly things in[100] the mountains. The worst thing was not being able to take a bath and get into her pajamas, but her mother told her it was[125] just for one night so they could sleep in their clothes.[136]

1. Where did Peewee want to take Lucy and her mother?
2. How will they cook their food?
3. What did Lucy think about bugs?
4. Why do you think her mom's boyfriend was called Peewee?
5. Why will they have to sleep on the ground?

Kate's grandmother was picking her up after school, and they were going to the animal shelter. Kate's dog, Baxter, had died last month, and Kate's[25] dad said she could get a new pet. The trouble was, Kate couldn't decide whether she wanted another dog or a cat. Her friend June[50] had a cat that was pretty cool. June's cat slept right next to her pillow every night and woke her up in the morning by[75] licking June's nose. Then again, Kate had really loved Baxter, who had played ball with her in the backyard and curled up on the couch[100] by her when she watched TV. Some dogs could even learn tricks, like rolling over or barking like they are singing. Kate decided she would[125] ask her grandmother if she thought dogs or cats were better pets.[137]

1. What was the name of Kate's dog?
2. Who was picking Kate up after school?
3. What did Baxter do when Kate watched TV?
4. Why wasn't Kate's dad taking her to the animal shelter?
5. How do you think Kate feels about getting a new pet?

Chad must have been daydreaming because Mr. Spurlock tapped him on the shoulder as he walked past his desk. Chad sighed as he realized Mr.[25] Spurlock was telling the class what their homework was for tonight. Chad felt like all he did after school was homework and more homework. It[50] seemed to take him forever to finish all of it. It seemed like the teachers gave more every day. Mr. Spurlock taught language arts, definitely[75] not Chad's favorite subject. He was supposed to be reading two chapters a night from a novel. Now Mr. Spurlock was giving a writing assignment![100] Chad's absolutely least favorite thing to do was writing. He couldn't seem to spell anything right. It made his hand hurt to write, and he[125] could never think of more than three sentences.[133]

1. What did Mr. Spurlock teach?
2. How many chapters was Chad supposed to read each night?
3. Why didn't Chad like to write?
4. Why doesn't Chad like language arts?
5. Why do you think it takes Chad such a long time to do his homework?

• •

Janet had a shoebox that she had covered in blue wrapping paper because blue was her favorite color. Janet kept this box hidden in her[25] closet under some old blankets. Janet made sure nobody was around when she got the blue box out of her closet. Janet liked to save[50] things in the box that helped her remember good times. She had the stub from the ticket when her aunt took her to see The[75] Nutcracker and the eye that had fallen off her teddy bear when she was little. She didn't have the bear anymore. The box also contained[100] every birthday card she had ever received and a tooth she had lost. Her favorite thing was a pinecone that she had found when hiking[125] with her dad.[128]

1. Where did Janet keep her special box?
2. Who took her to see The Nutcracker?
3. Why did Janet cover the box with blue paper?
4. Why did Janet keep the box hidden?
5. Why do you think the pinecone was her favorite thing?

Pete and Luke thought they were lucky to live where they did. Their house was at the end of the street, and the only thing[25] next to their house was a wooded area with tall oaks and pine trees. Deep inside the woods was a small pond complete with tadpoles[50] in the spring that became croaking frogs by summer. In the summer, when the days were long, Pete and Luke loved to play in the[75] woods. They would get up early in the morning and pack their backpacks with peanut butter and jelly sandwiches, cookies, and juice boxes. Then the[100] boys would head into the woods and climb trees or play hide-and-seek. They would swing on vines that hung from the tall trees. When it[125] was really hot, they would take off their shoes and hang their feet in the pond while they ate their lunch.[146]

1. What was in the pond during the springtime?
2. What did the boys put in their backpacks?
3. Where were the woods?
4. Why aren't there any tadpoles in the summer?
5. Why did Pete and Luke put their feet in the pond on hot days?

1 Ann's Mother Gets to Vote

Ann and her family lived on a small, isolated farm in Wyoming, their nearest neighbors almost ten miles away. The closest city was Cody, where[25] Ann's mother was the schoolteacher. Ann liked having her own mother as her teacher because she could get assistance with her homework whenever she needed[50] it. Ann's mother was very excited because it was Election Day! Ann's mother took Ann with her to the courthouse in Cody where people were[75] lining up to cast their votes for mayor and president of the United States. Last year on Election Day, only Ann's father and the other[100] men had gone to town to vote, but this year was different. Wyoming, a state full of cowboys and ranchers, had decided that women could[125] vote too. Ann's mother, some women from the bank, and some of the other ladies joined the line and talked quietly about the men who[150] were running for office. They were ready to cast their votes in this historic event.[165]

1. What town is near Ann's farm?
2. What job does Ann's mother have?
3. Where did Ann and her mother go this morning?
4. Why might someone not like to have her own mother as her teacher?
5. Why didn't Ann's mother vote last year?

. . . .

Tom's favorite thing to do was go to work with his father, though of course, Tom couldn't do this during the school year. Tom's father[25] unloaded cargo from ships that had arrived in Boston from ports around the globe. Because his father often had to work late into the evening,[50] he didn't get to eat dinner with his family. Instead, Tom's mother would send Tom to the docks to bring his father dinner. Tom loved[75] running through the streets with the sack of food, taking in the sights around him as he went. Tom ran so the food would still[100] be warm when he got to the dock, knowing that his father would take a break when he got there and share his dinner with[125] him. Tonight was a cold night in December, so Tom ran extra fast to keep warm. When he got to the dock, he was surprised[150] to see a lot of men dressed up like Indians climbing aboard the ships and dumping something into the water. It looked like they were[175] dumping huge chests of tea into the water. Tom was concerned because he didn't see his father anywhere.[193]

1. Where did Tom's father work?
2. What did Tom take to his father at work?
3. What surprised Tom when he got to the dock on this night?
4. Why might the food be cold when Tom gets to the dock tonight?
5. Why do you think Tom couldn't find his father?

3 | Susan Meets Stevie

Like most kids in the 1960s, Susan had a small radio called a transistor radio or a pocket radio. Her transistor radio was bright red,[25] got all of her favorite stations, and was rarely found anywhere but in Susan's pocket or purse. Susan and three of her friends, also big[50] music fans, were excited because Susan's mother was taking them to the taping of a radio show. They would get to see the performance live[75] and perhaps even meet the entertainer. When they arrived at the station, the girls hurried into the studio where the show would be taped and[100] saw the musician sitting at the piano warming up. The girls were puzzled to see that he was wearing sunglasses, though there was certainly no[125] sun in the darkened studio. Susan approached the singer, autograph book in hand, a bit nervous but excited as well. The singer didn't appear to[150] be that much older than Susan and her friends. When he heard Susan approaching, he turned and introduced himself as Stevie. He signed her book[175] and invited her to sit next to him on the piano bench and play a few notes.[192]

1. What color was Susan's small radio?
2. Who was taking Susan and her friends to the radio show?
3. What instrument was the singer playing?
4. Why might the singer be wearing sunglasses?
5. Why might a transistor radio also be called a pocket radio?

4 Russ Helps the Family Pack

• •

It had been another dismal year for Russ and his family in Oklahoma where his father was a farmer who tried to grow corn and[25] wheat. The attempt was not successful, however, because for the second year in a row, nothing grew. The crops of all the farmers in the[50] region had died because it never rained, and the ground was as dry as it had ever been. The crops could not be expected to[75] survive in such dire conditions. Dust blew into your eyes when you went outside, making you close your eyes and feel your way around. Now[100] the family was moving back to Tennessee where they could stay with Russ's grandfather. Russ helped his father lift the last chair onto the back[125] of the truck, and then they put the boxes with the pots and pans in too. His mother carried out some blankets and his baby[150] sister who was scared and crying. The heavy woolen blankets went into the back of the truck before the whole family crowded into the front[175] seat for the long and dusty drive back East.[184]

1. What crops did his father try to grow?
2. What things were Russ and his father packing in the truck?
3. What is Russ's mom carrying?
4. Why did Russ's family have to move back to Tennessee?
5. How do you think Russ feels about moving to Tennessee?

5 Liz Dreams Big

. . . .

Things were quite different for girls in the 1800s compared to girls going to school in the 21st century. More than a century ago, girls[25] were not permitted to do many things that boys could do, though they were certainly capable. Elizabeth and her friends loved to pretend they were[50] grown up. When they did this, some of Elizabeth's friends pretended to be teachers or shopkeepers, bankers or seamstresses. These were occupations that were currently[75] held by women and were familiar to the young girls of that day. These jobs were never Elizabeth's choice when she pretended to be an[100] adult, though. Whenever she played pretend, she chose to be a doctor, perhaps because her grandfather was a doctor. Elizabeth loved to travel with him[125] when he visited his patients, and she even had a little black case that her grandfather had given her. In it she had collected what[150] she considered to be some things doctors might use. She had the old bottles from pills and even some scissors and a saw he no[175] longer used, though she didn't really want to know what the saw was for.[189]

1. Who did Elizabeth know who was a doctor?
2. What did Elizabeth's friends pretend to be?
3. What did Elizabeth keep her doctor things in?
4. What do you think Elizabeth wanted to be when she grew up?
5. Why would a doctor use a saw?

Although young Billy was opposed to the idea of leaving New York, he had little choice as his father was determined to move West. New[25] York was the only place Billy had ever lived, and he couldn't imagine anywhere else feeling like home. He and his family were not moving[50] just a short distance, but they were going to travel almost the entire length of the country to a place called New Mexico. Billy's father[75] said he wanted to give the family a fresh start, and getting as far away from New York was the best way to do that.[100] Billy had gotten into trouble more than once at his old school in New York, earning him the nickname of Bad Boy Bonney. His father[125] tried to convince Billy that he would like New Mexico where they would have a farm with horses and cattle, and Billy could learn to[150] ride, rope the cattle, and build fences. When he was a little older, his father would teach him how to shoot a gun. Billy had[175] to admit that sounded like it might be interesting, and he thought that maybe the move out West was a good idea. He just hoped[200] his nickname didn't follow him to his new school.[209]

1. Where did Billy live until the move?
2. What animals will the family have in New Mexico?
3. What was Billy's nickname in New York?
4. Why do you think he had that nickname?
5. Why did Billy decide moving out West might be all right after all?

Maria's Neighbor Is a Pioneer

Maria's neighbor, Christa, who was a teacher at the high school, told Maria that she would be gone for several months. Maria really liked Christa[25] and wondered what would take her away for so long. Christa seemed excited as she explained to Maria and her mother that she had been[50] selected to train to be an astronaut and go into outer space. Maria had watched some of the space shuttles take off on TV and[75] was proud that her neighbor would join this elite group of space travelers. While in space, Christa would have to wear a special suit, and[100] if she went outside the spacecraft, she would have to wear a helmet that was connected by a tube to the spaceship. There was no[125] oxygen in space, and this tube allowed the astronauts to breathe. Maria had seen that you could float in the air inside the spaceship. Maria[150] thought her neighbor was lucky to have such an opportunity.[160]

1. What was Maria's neighbor going to do?
2. What do astronauts have to wear if they go outside the spaceship?
3. How did Maria's neighbor feel about going into space?
4. Why do astronauts have to be connected to the spaceship by a tube if they go outside?
5. Why would Christa have to be gone for months if the space mission was just a few days long?

In a small town in Ohio, called Dayton, lived a curious young girl named Amy. Next door to her, in a rambling house with blue[25] shutters and a red door, lived two brothers who were always building something, and this fascinated Amy. One of the previous ventures of the creative[50] brothers was making bicycles, and Amy had seen them riding on these special bikes many times. She had looked at the bicycles in the window[75] of the store owned by the brothers, but they were much too expensive for Amy to have one! One summer her neighbors built a very[100] odd-looking kite that flew high and stayed aloft a surprisingly long time. Their latest invention was a strange-looking machine much bigger than a kite that[125] was supposed to fly! She wasn't sure how that was going to work because their glider looked nothing like a bird or a kite. It[150] had two wings on top of each other. Amy loved to watch the brothers build things and talk about their inventions, dreaming that someday she[175] might also invent something.[179]

1. Where did Amy live?
2. Why didn't Amy have one of the brothers' bicycles?
3. Why did Amy think the glider wouldn't fly?
4. Why do you think Amy liked to watch the brothers work?
5. Why don't the brothers make bicycles any more?

9 Rosa Goes to School

On school days, Rosa walked to school along the hot and dusty dirt road with her mother, who was a teacher at the school. Rosa[25] went to a school where all the grades were in one room, called a one-room schoolhouse. Rosa liked her teacher, Miss Hill, as much as[50] she had ever liked any teacher. Rosa's favorite thing to do was read, perhaps because Rosa's mother had taught her how to read before she[75] started school. Miss Hill, also an avid reader, brought in many different books for the students to read, and she was delighted to help them[100] select one to take home. Rosa and the other students at her school only went to school five months out of the year, while white[125] students at the other schools went for nine months. Rosa and the other black students had to help on the farm when it was time[150] to plant or harvest, and this limited the time for their education.[162]

1. What was Rosa's favorite thing to do?
2. Why did Rosa go to school only five months of the year?
3. What was Rosa's mother's job?
4. Why did Rosa like her teacher?
5. Why were white students allowed to go to school for nine months?

••

The excitement was too much for Jess, so he gave up trying to sleep and got up very early in the morning. His famous uncle[25] George, whom he hadn't seen in nearly five years, was coming to visit his family. The whole family had moved to South Dakota about a[50] year ago so Jess's dad could be a miner. Uncle George, his dad's brother, was a general in the army. Although he had been stationed[75] in the Black Hills of South Dakota for several years, he hadn't been able to take time off for a visit until now. After his[100] visit with Jess and the family, Uncle George and his men would depart for a mission to Montana. Uncle George had written them a letter[125] explaining that he and his men were being assigned to a dangerous mission to explore the area near the Little Big Horn in the spring.[150] Uncle George always had great stories to tell, so Jess knew this visit would be another interesting one. He eagerly awaited Uncle George's arrival, hoping[175] that he would also bring him a souvenir from his travels.[186]

1. Where does Jess live?
2. What is Jess's uncle's name?
3. To what state is Uncle George going after the visit?
4. What might be dangerous about the mission to explore Little Big Horn?
5. Why did Uncle George have great stories to tell?

1 Floods

· ·

Water falls from clouds and is absorbed in the soil or fills rivers. Then it evaporates and returns to the clouds. Floods occur when there[25] is too much water in the soil and rivers. Lots of things can cause this imbalance. Heavy rainfall or lots of snow melting can cause[50] too much water to build up in lakes, rivers, and streams. Soil that is already too saturated from heavy rain can't hold any more water.[75] There are two basic types of floods. In a regular flood, a river gets fuller and fuller and then overflows its banks. The more dangerous[100] type of flood is a flash flood. This occurs when a wall of water quickly sweeps over an area of land. Up until now, scientists[125] haven't been very good at predicting when and where flash floods will occur. This is changing because of a tool called Doppler radar.[148]

1. Name two things that can cause too much water in lakes or rivers.
2. What are the two basic types of floods?
3. What new tool are scientists using to predict flash floods?
4. Why doesn't it flood every time it rains?
5. Why are flash floods more dangerous than regular floods?

2 Wildfires

Wildfires start outdoors in wooded areas or on the plains and often occur when it has been a dry season. Lightning or a careless person[25] who throws out a match or cigarette may start a wildfire. A person may also start a wildfire on purpose during a crime. This is[50] called arson. When the wind blows, wildfires can spread very fast. Houses in the area are in danger of burning. In places that are prone[75] to wildfires, people should keep an area around their houses clear of trees. This may lessen the chance that a fire will spread to a[100] house. During a large wildfire, firefighters from many states may be called in to help fight the fire. The main tool used to fight wildfires[125] is the fire plow, not water. The firefighters use the plow to dig a trench that the fire cannot cross. Sometimes helicopters are used to[150] drop large buckets of water on the fire.[158]

1. How can a wildfire start?
2. What is the crime called when someone starts a fire on purpose?
3. What makes wildfires spread so fast?
4. Why are there more wildfires in a dry season?
5. Why can't firefighters use hoses attached to hydrants to fight the wildfires?

3   Ice Storms

· ·

A rainstorm can suddenly turn into an ice storm if the temperature drops. Rain begins to freeze on the branches of trees, on cars, and[25] on power lines. The frozen branches make it look like a winter wonderland. The branches glisten in the light and make crackling noises when they[50] touch together. However, as more and more ice forms on the branches, they become heavy. They may become so heavy that they break off from[75] the trees and crash to the ground. They can damage property or injure people. When ice forms on power lines, they can break loose from[100] the poles. Then houses lose power and the electricity goes out. Houses are dark and cold. It can sometimes take days or weeks for the[125] power company to fix all the damage and restore power.[135]

1. What causes a rainstorm to change into an ice storm?
2. On what does the ice form during such a storm?
3. What happens when the electricity goes out?
4. How can an ice storm harm people?
5. Why does it sometimes take a long time for the power company to restore power?

4 Earthquakes

• •

An earthquake is the sudden shaking and rolling of the surface of the earth. Earthquakes happen along fault lines, cracks deep under the surface of[25] the earth. Most earthquakes last less than one minute. Earthquakes, unlike other disasters, are not related to weather. An earthquake could occur on a clear,[50] sunny day. California and Nevada are at high risk for earthquakes. There is also an area in the Midwest along the Mississippi River that is[75] prone to quakes. After an earthquake stops, there is more shaking coming. These are smaller quakes called aftershocks. The severity of earthquakes is measured on[100] a scale. Severe earthquakes can be felt for thousands of miles. They can cause houses to fall. If you are ever in an earthquake, you[125] should drop to the ground. Get under something to keep falling objects from hitting you, and hold on![143]

1. What is a fault line?
2. How long do most earthquakes last?
3. Name a state that has many earthquakes.
4. Why do you think you should drop to the ground during an earthquake?
5. Why aren't earthquakes related to the weather?

5 Drought

• •

A drought is not simply a lack of rainfall. Drought occurs when there is much less rainfall than predicted. This occurs over a long period[25] of time. During a drought, farmers are affected. There is no rain to water their crops. If they use an irrigation system for watering, there[50] may not be enough water in the lakes to use for irrigation. There are direct and indirect effects of droughts. A direct effect is the[75] farmer not having enough water for his crops. An indirect effect is the farmer not having enough money to buy new clothes for his children[100] or a new tractor. During a drought, people in cities may be told they cannot water their grass or trees. In some countries, drought can[125] result in a severe food shortage. Drought can be caused by a lack of rainfall or snowfall.[142]

1. What is a drought?
2. How are people in cities affected by drought?
3. What causes a drought?
4. What happens to crops during a drought?
5. During a drought, why wouldn't a farmer have enough money for a new tractor?

6 Lightning

· ·

There doesn't need to be a major storm for lightning to strike. Lightning may be pretty to look at, but it can be deadly. Lightning[25] in the United States kills almost a hundred people a year. The best place to be during a lightning storm is inside a building. However,[50] even inside a building you have to be careful. You should not be near windows or doors, phone lines or power lines. A car with[75] a metal roof also offers protection, as long as you are not touching any metal part of the car that leads to the outside. Do[100] you know the 30/30 rule for staying safe around lightning? If you see lightning, count the seconds until you hear thunder. If the number[125] is 30 seconds or less, you should go inside. Stay there until 30 minutes after the last thunder or lightning flash.[146]

1. How many people in the U.S. die from lightning strikes each year?
2. Where is the safest place to be during a lightning storm?
3. How long should you stay inside after a storm?
4. Why do you think you shouldn't touch metal parts of the car that lead to the outside?
5. Why is it called the 30/30 rule?

Hail can be a very damaging part of a storm. Hail usually occurs in storms from super cells. Rain falling through a super cell picks[25] up more and more layers of water. The rotating air in the super cell takes the hail up and down many times before it finally[50] falls to the ground. This recycling of the hail might last five to ten minutes. This allows the hail to get very large. Once the[75] hail is too heavy to be held up by the winds, it falls to the earth at speeds of 100 miles per hour. Hail can[100] be small like a pea or extremely large like a baseball. The record for the biggest hailstone belongs to a town in Nebraska, where a[125] few years ago, a hailstone was measured to be seven inches in diameter. This hail left a crater-sized hole when it hit. Hail of a[150] much smaller size can do serious damage to crops, cars, and people.[162]

1. What keeps hail from falling straight to the ground while it is still small?
2. How long can a hailstone keep recycling before falling to the ground?
3. How fast can a hailstone fall?
4. Since the size of hail is described by comparing it to common objects, how would you describe the size of the record hailstone?
5. How does hail damage crops?

8 Blizzards

• •

A blizzard is a winter storm that has lots of blowing snow and winds. It does not have to snow heavily or be extremely cold[25] to be considered a blizzard. The strong winds can even pick up snow that has already fallen and make a blizzard. Blizzards can be very[50] dangerous if you are traveling in a car. The blowing snow makes it very difficult for the driver to see. The high winds in a[75] blizzard make it dangerous to be outside. The wind makes the air feel much colder. This is reported as a wind chill factor. A fifteen-mile[100] per hour wind can make a temperature of zero feel like it is really 36 degrees below zero. People who are outside in bitter cold[125] can suffer from frostbite. Frostbite can damage body tissue.[134]

1. Why is it dangerous to drive a car during a blizzard?
2. What is a wind chill factor?
3. What can happen to your fingers if you are outside too long when it is really cold?
4. How could people find out that a blizzard might occur so that they can stay inside?
5. What could a driver do if he were caught driving during a blizzard?

9 Hurricanes

We give hurricanes names to help us track them as they move across the ocean. There can be more than one hurricane at a time.[25] Giving them names helps us keep them straight. In 1953, the U.S. National Weather Service began using female names for these storms. In 1979, they[50] started using men's names too. The Weather Service has six lists of names they rotate and use to name storms. The list they use this[75] year will be used again in six years. The only time a name is removed from the list is if a hurricane is very deadly[100] or costly. Then its name is retired and a new name is chosen. Over 50 hurricane names are retired. Hurricane Katrina hit the Gulf Coast[125] in 2005. It is the deadliest hurricane in U.S. history. Over 1,000 people died, many when the levees surrounding New Orleans broke and the city[150] was flooded.[152]

1. Why do we give hurricanes names?
2. How many lists of names are there?
3. How many hurricane names are retired?
4. Why do you think the name Katrina will be retired?
5. Why do you think the U.S. National Weather Service started using men's names as well as women's names for these storms?

10 Tornadoes

● ●

Tornadoes can form at any time of the year, but they happen a lot in the spring. Tornadoes can happen anywhere. In the United States,[25] there is an area called Tornado Alley. This area, from Texas to the Dakotas, has more tornadoes than other parts of the country. Tornadoes can[50] form out of any type of storm, but most form from a storm called a super cell. A super cell has air that spins and[75] can become a tornado. Winds from a tornado can top 300 miles per hour. A tornado can only be called a tornado if it touches[100] the ground. If it does not, it is called a funnel cloud. Almost 1,000 tornadoes are reported in the United States each year. Scientists use[125] a special scale to rank the severity of a tornado. The levels range from a zero to a five.[144]

1. How fast can winds in a tornado be?
2. What kind of storm often spawns a tornado?
3. How many tornadoes are reported in the U.S. each year?
4. Why do you think a lot of tornadoes occur in the spring?
5. Why do you think the word "alley" is used to describe the area of the U.S. that has the most tornadoes?

1   **Martha Dandridge Custis Washington**

Martha Washington was the first of the First Ladies. She did not entirely enjoy the role. Martha had experienced many hardships before she became First[25] Lady. She had married when she was eighteen years old. After losing two children, she became a widow. Soon after, she married George Washington. She[50] worried greatly about her husband during the Revolutionary War and would have preferred a private life. However, she understood when George accepted what he viewed[75] as his duty to lead the country. She and George lived in temporary capitals in New York and Philadelphia. They entertained in formal style. Her[100] guests commented that Martha always made them feel at ease. She was probably the happiest when she and George retired from public life. They returned[125] to live at Mount Vernon. She enjoyed life there surrounded by her grandchildren. She and George are buried at Mount Vernon. Much more could be[150] known about Martha and George had she not burned their letters.[161]

    1. How old was Martha when she first married?

    2. Where did she and George live during his presidency?

    3. Where did George and Martha live after they retired?

    4. Why did Martha worry about George during the Revolutionary War?

    5. Why do you think Martha burned their letters?

2 Edith Kermit Carow Roosevelt

There were two Roosevelt First Ladies, and the lesser known was Edith. She and Teddy had known each other their entire lives. As a child,[25] Edith was a playmate of Teddy's younger sister. Edith grew up on Union Square in New York and attended a finishing school. This was typical[50] for young ladies from wealthy families of that era. She attended Teddy's first wedding to Alice Hathaway. Alice died, leaving Teddy with a young daughter,[75] also named Alice. A year later, Edith married Teddy. They lived in a house called Sagamore Hill. Their family quickly grew, with five more children[100] born in the next ten years. A tragedy brought them to the White House when President McKinley was assassinated. Edith was a skillful entertainer, a[125] trait required of First Ladies. Later in life, after Teddy had died, Edith traveled to Europe and continued her charity work. She worked with a[150] group that provided clothing for the poor.[157]

1. Who was Edith's childhood playmate?
2. Where did Edith grow up?
3. What was the name of the house where Edith and Teddy lived?
4. How many children in all were part of Edith and Teddy's family?
5. Why did Teddy become president after McKinley was assassinated?

3 Frances Folsom Cleveland

Frances Folsom was a talented college graduate. She loved to read, spoke French and German, and read Latin. She enjoyed taking pictures as a hobby.[25] Before his death, Frances's father had been a law partner with Grover Cleveland. After Frances's father died, she and her mother often visited with President[50] Cleveland. Frances was much younger than the president, so it was a surprise to many when she became engaged to him. She was the first[75] woman to marry a president in his first term in the White House. The wedding took place in the Blue Room. The press was very[100] taken with Frances, nicknamed "Frankie." In fact, the press bothered the president and Frances so much that sometimes they moved out of the White House[125] and stayed in a home a few miles away. Frankie was probably the first First Lady to receive such attention from the press. Cleveland lost[150] the election in 1888, but he and Frankie were back in the White House four years later.[167]

1. What happened to Frances's father?
2. What languages did Frances speak?
3. Where did her wedding take place?
4. Why do you think the press was so interested in Frankie?
5. Why did they move back into the White House four years later?

4 Jacqueline Lee Bouvier Kennedy

Jackie was born to wealth and raised with all its benefits. She attended the best schools and grew up in several beautiful homes. As a[25] college student, she spent a year in France, sparking her interest in citizens of foreign countries. She took a job as a photographer for a[50] paper in Washington, D.C. While there, she met Senator Kennedy. Their marriage seemed to many like a fairy tale, but Jackie suffered her share of[75] heartaches. She lost three children. The last died just a few days after his birth. The nation mourned with the First Family. Jackie had a[100] great interest in the arts, sparking a national interest in culture. She worked to make the White House something of a museum. When her husband[125] was assassinated, she was described as courageous. One of the more compelling pictures in history is of Jackie standing beside Lyndon Johnson on Air Force[150] One as he is sworn in as president.[158]

1. Where did Jackie study abroad?

2. What was her first job?

3. Who became president after Kennedy was assassinated?

4. Why did the Kennedy marriage seem like a fairy tale?

5. Why do you think Jackie was described as courageous after her husband was assassinated?

5   Hillary Rodham Clinton

• •

A modern-day First Lady, Hillary was often as visible as the president. She had her own career before she married Bill. She was an excellent[25] student and a leader involved in student government. After graduating from law school, she worked for a while in Boston and Washington, D.C., before moving[50] to Arkansas. There she married Bill and worked as a lawyer and taught in law school. After he became governor, she balanced her duties as[75] Arkansas' First Lady with her public service work. She served prominent roles during Bill's term as president. She chaired the Task Force on National Health[100] Care Reform. She received some criticism for her visible role. She was a strong supporter of women's and children's rights. She wrote a best-selling novel.[125] It is entitled *It Takes a Village*. She also won a Grammy for her recording of this book. After Bill left office, Hillary became the[150] first First Lady elected to the United States Senate.[159]

1. What was Hillary's job before Bill became governor?
2. In which state was Bill the governor?
3. Why did Hillary win a Grammy?
4. What kind of grades do you think Hillary got in school?
5. Why is Hillary described as a modern-day First Lady?

6 Julia Dent Grant

Perhaps the most interesting part of Julia Grant's life was the period before Ulysses assumed the presidency. Julia and Ulysses, who was in the army,[25] became engaged in 1844. However, they had to wait four years through the Mexican War before they could marry. After their marriage, Julia followed Ulysses[50] to many military posts. She had to return home in 1852 when he was sent to the West. He resigned from the army two years[75] later to be with Julia and their children. He tried many business ventures in St. Louis, none of them successful. The Grants then returned to[100] Illinois. Ulysses worked for his father in a leather goods store. The Grants might have lived the rest of their lives there, but the Civil[125] War began. Ulysses was called to duty. Once more, Julia was apart from her husband. She tried to meet him when she could. After living[150] such a hard life, it must have been a wonderful time for Julia serving as First Lady.[167]

1. What did Ulysses do before he became President?
2. What war caused a delay in the Grants being able to marry?
3. Why did Ulysses resign from the army?
4. How do you think Julia felt when Ulysses was away?
5. Why did Julia and Ulysses leave St. Louis and move back to Illinois?

Dolley Payne Todd Madison

Dolley Madison is perhaps one of the best known of the First
Ladies. Dolley was born in North Carolina and lived there as a child.[25]
Dolley's father moved the family to Philadelphia when Dolley was a
young woman. Dolley was raised as a Quaker. Like other women of
her time,[50] she married young, had a child, and became a widow. She
had experienced all of this before the age of twenty-five. Dolley was an
outgoing[75] woman. She soon began dating James Madison from Virginia.
After her marriage to James, she stopped dressing like a Quaker and
instead wore the best[100] fashions. She was sometimes described as
looking like a queen. Throughout Madison's political career, Dolley was
known for her skillful entertaining. It is less well-known[125] that she was
also helpful to her husband in dealing with political issues. The Madisons
had to flee the White House in 1812. They returned[150] to find it burned
to the ground. This did not stop Dolley who was able to entertain in
temporary quarters.[170]

1. When did Dolley move to Philadelphia?
2. In what religion was Dolley raised?
3. Where was James Madison from?
4. Why do you think it was common at the time for people,
   like Dolley's first husband, to die young?
5. Why do you think Dolley decided to keep entertaining
   after the White House was burned?

8 Lou Henry Hoover

Lou was an outdoors person, skilled in horseback riding and hunting. She was also skilled as a taxidermist. As a teen, her favorite pastime was[25] to go camping with her father. On these camping trips, she developed an interest in rocks and mining. She met Herbert at Stanford University when[50] she was a freshman and he was a senior. After she graduated, they married and began to travel. Herbert was a mining engineer, and he[75] became a millionaire from this work. His career took them to places such as Egypt, Japan, and China. Lou had two sons who were born[100] during these travels. While in China, the Boxer Rebellion broke out. Lou worked in hospitals there while Herbert helped build barricades. During World War I,[125] Lou was often with Herbert when he administered programs to provide emergency aid. Lou was very involved in the Girl Scouts, even serving as its[150] president. During Herbert's term as president, the country suffered from a great depression. The Hoovers often used their own money to entertain.[172]

1. What was Lou's favorite thing to do as a teen?
2. What did Lou do while she was in China?
3. For which organization did Lou serve as president?
4. What do you think Lou might have done with the animals she killed when hunting?
5. Why did the Hoover's use their own money to entertain while in the White House?

Unlike many First Ladies, Rosalynn came from a humble beginning. Her father died when she was thirteen. Her mother became a dressmaker to support the[25] family. Rosalynn worked with her mother in this endeavor. Like many other First Ladies, her husband was in the armed services. Jimmy served in the[50] navy. This meant the family moved around a lot. Rosalynn was a tireless campaigner for her husband. She often traveled on her own to meet[75] voters. As First Lady, she had two diverse interests. She increased awareness of the performing arts, inviting many artists to perform in the White House.[100] This included the first large scale jazz production on the White House lawn. She also championed an effort to help people better understand mental health[125] disorders. She and Jimmy may have accomplished more in the years since the presidency. They work tirelessly to promote peace and human rights around the[150] world. She also continues to work to help people understand mental illness.[162]

1. How did Rosalynn's mother support her family?
2. What kind of music was performed on the White House lawn?
3. How old was Rosalynn when her father died?
4. Why did the jazz production occur on the White House lawn?
5. Why do families in the armed services move around a lot?

Perhaps the First Lady with the most unusual name was Lady Bird Johnson. She was never called by her given name, Claudia. Her mother died[25] when she was only five years old, so her father and an aunt raised her. She was perhaps a more involved wife than many others.[50] When Lyndon went to fight in World War II, Lady Bird worked to keep his congressional office open. When he had a heart attack, she[75] helped keep things running until he could return to the Senate. She was also a more visible and active First Lady than others. Her main[100] interest was the environment. She began this interest in Washington with the First Lady's Committee for a More Beautiful Capital. It was Lady Bird who[125] spearheaded the campaign to stop littering. She was very involved in Lyndon's program called the War on Poverty. She was interested in the Head Start[150] program. After returning to Texas, she maintained her interest in the environment. There she started a program called the National Wildflower Research Center.[173]

1. How old was Lady Bird when her mother died?
2. How did Lady Bird help when Lyndon had a heart attack?
3. What was Lady Bird's main interest?
4. How is littering related to Lady Bird's interest in the environment?
5. How do you think it affected Lady Bird to lose her mother?

Alan grew up in a loving home environment in quiet Cody, Wyoming. That didn't stop his friends and him from finding ways to get into[25] trouble. As a youth, Alan was known for having a temper. He threw rocks at other children, and as a teen, he graduated to stealing[50] rifle shells to play a dangerous game with guns. On one outing, he and his friends shot holes in mailboxes. The local authorities figured out[75] who had done this, and since mailboxes are considered federal property, Alan found himself in federal court. He pled guilty and was given two years[100] probation. His probation officer, J.B. Mosely, had a significant impact on Alan. Alan went on to college and law school. As a young lawyer, he[125] often defended juvenile delinquents. He dealt with them using tough, honest talk. He served in the state legislature. Eventually, Alan took over his father's Senate[150] seat. During his 18 years in the Senate, he held the second highest leadership position in the Republican Party.[169]

1. What was one of the earliest things Alan did to get in trouble?
2. Who had an impact on helping Alan turn his life around?
3. How long did Alan serve in the U.S. Senate?
4. Why would mailboxes be considered federal property?
5. How do you think Alan's parents felt about his troubles with the law?

• •

Paul remembers being in second grade and still not knowing the letters of the alphabet when all of the other students in the class were[25] already reading. He didn't learn to read until he was in junior high, and even then he could barely keep up. He was a terrible[50] speller and sometimes failed tests just because he spelled so many words wrong. He worked in his father's factory after school, but quit when one[75] of the other workers told other people he couldn't read. When one of his teachers in college found out that Paul had a learning disability,[100] he started looking past Paul's poor spelling to see the brilliant ideas in his writing. While in college, Paul started his business in a rented[125] garage. He sold pens and notebooks and had a small copy machine. Some days he made $1000! His business grew and grew. The name of[150] his business, Kinko's, is based on the nickname he earned because he has curly hair. Now there are over 800 Kinko's stores around the world.[175] Paul is still not a good reader, but he has found a way to be very successful in the world of business.[197]

1. How old was Paul when he began to learn how to read?
2. Where did he work after school?
3. How did his company get the name Kinko's?
4. How do you think Paul felt when his college professor said he had brilliant ideas?
5. How might Paul's life have been different if he didn't have a learning disability?

Can you imagine growing up in a house without electricity? There was no TV, microwave, or radio in the log cabin where Jewel grew up[25] in Alaska with her parents. Despite her dyslexia, Jewel began writing poetry when she was six years old. When her parents divorced, she lived with[50] her dad and her brothers and started singing with her father at local hotels. She really missed her mother and went to Hawaii for a[75] while to get away from the stress, but she soon returned to Alaska. She wanted to go to a special high school for fine arts[100] in Michigan, but her parents couldn't afford the tuition. She was determined to be an artist, so she played benefit concerts and raised the money[125] herself. After she finished school, she moved to San Diego. She lived out of her old VW van and sang on street corners for change.[150] Her big break came when a record company executive heard her and signed her to a record contract with Atlantic Records. She sold eight million[175] copies of her debut album. She also writes poetry and has published a book of her poems.[192]

1. In which state did Jewel grow up?
2. What kind of house did Jewel live in?
3. How did she afford the special art school in Michigan?
4. Why do you think Jewel came back from Hawaii?
5. Why do you think Jewel lived in her van in California?

Nancy Lopez

• •

Nancy got her first set of golf clubs when she was only eight, and two years later she won the state championship. Her father so[25] believed in her talent that he dug a hole in the backyard and filled it with sand so she could practice hitting balls out of[50] the sand trap. When she was in high school, there wasn't a women's golf team so she played on the team with the men, helping[75] them win two state championships. As a Mexican- American, she faced discrimination because of her culture. Her family was not allowed to join the country club[100] where they lived. Before Nancy turned pro, her mother died of a heart attack. As a pro, she was named Rookie of the Year and[125] won many tournaments. By the age of 30, she was inducted into the LPGA Hall of Fame. In 2000, during the LPGA's 50th anniversary, she[150] was recognized as one of the 50 best players and teachers. She is now a spokesperson for prevention of heart disease and stroke.[173]

   1. Why did Nancy's father dig a hole in their backyard?

   2. Why did Nancy play on the men's team in high school?

   3. How old was Nancy when she was inducted into the Hall of Fame?

   4. What award did Nancy win her first year as pro?

   5. Why do you think Nancy is a spokesperson for the prevention of heart disease?

5 Gloria Steinem

Gloria had an interesting start to her childhood. She credits these experiences in helping her form her views of life. Gloria did not attend school[25] until she was 12 years old. Instead, she traveled around the country with her parents in a house trailer as they bought and sold antiques.[50] They believed this travel and exposure to different parts of the country were as educational as any school. When she was enrolled in school, she[75] found the adjustment difficult. Gloria attended college on a scholarship. She was politically active in college. After graduating, she went to India to study for[100] two years. When she returned, she could not find a job as a journalist because editors wanted to hire men. She became a freelance writer.[125] As a writer, she covered political campaigns, among other things. She became active in the feminist movement. She was a co-founder of the National Women's[150] Political Caucus. In 1972, she founded the feminist magazine Ms.[160]

1. Why didn't Gloria go to school until she was 12 years old?
2. In what foreign country did Gloria study?
3. Why did Gloria's parents travel around the country?
4. Why would it be difficult to start going to school at age 12?
5. How could travel be as educational as school?

6 Richard Branson

••

Richard found school to be a nightmare. His dyslexia that required him to try to memorize words embarrassed him. As a teen, he was frustrated[25] with the rigid school rules. He became involved in student activism. He and a friend formed a newspaper, not just for their school, but also[50] to tie together many schools. They sold ads to corporations, worked out of the basement to save on other costs, and launched the successful paper,[75] Student. Richard's next business success came when he started a discount record business, even though he had no experience. He and his friends found an[100] empty shop above a shoe store. Instead of paying rent, they promised the owner of the shoe store that so many people would come to[125] buy records that sales in the shoe store would also increase. They named the record business Virgin, and the rest is history! There are now[150] over 150 different types of businesses with the Virgin name ranging from Virgin Airlines to Virgin Cola.[167]

1. What was the name of the newspaper Richard started while in school?
2. How did Richard and his friend pay for the cost of the newspaper?
3. Where was Richard's record store located?
4. Why would more people coming to the record store help sales in the shoe store downstairs?
5. Why do you think Richard had the courage to start a record business when he had no experience?

Oprah was not born to the wealth she now knows. She was born in Mississippi, and when her parents separated, they sent her to live[25] in poor surroundings with her grandmother. She later lived with her mother and then her father. She suffered abuse for years, and as a teen,[50] she struggled with drugs and acting out. What seemed to turn things around for Oprah was winning a scholarship to a university. She was a[75] bright student with an interest in journalism. She landed a job at a television station and became the first African-American woman to work as a[100] news anchor in Nashville. Her career really took off when she moved to Chicago to host a morning TV talk show. Shortly after, the name[125] of the show was changed to The Oprah Winfrey Show. In 1996, she began to have an incredible influence on the reading habits of the[150] American people. She established Oprah's Book Club and endorsed books she considered to have value. The books she selected often jumped to number one on[175] the best-seller list.[178]

1. What kind of trouble was Oprah in as a teenager?
2. What helped Oprah turn her life around?
3. In what city is her talk show?
4. Why did books Oprah picked for her book club top the best-seller list?
5. How do we know Oprah's morning talk show was a success?

8 Bob Beamon

• •

Bob Beamon grew up poor in New York, never knowing his parents. He was raised by a stepfather who ended up in prison. His grandmother,[25] Bessie, did her best to raise Bob. She held a job as a domestic worker to put food on the table, but she did not[50] provide much supervision. Bob was already getting into trouble by the age of nine, skipping school, stealing, and getting into fights. This continued for years,[75] and at age 14, he ran away from home and joined a gang. When a fight at school resulted in an injury to a teacher,[100] Bob found himself in juvenile court, faced with being sent to a detention facility. When his grandmother agreed to take more responsibility, the judge instead[125] sent Bob to an alternative school. Bob later returned to his own high school and began to excel at track, setting many records. His crowning[150] achievement came in the 1968 Olympics when he set a world record in the long jump that would stand for 23 years. He beat the[175] previous record by an amazing two feet![182]

1. How old was Bob when he began to get into trouble?
2. Where did Bob grow up?
3. How long did the Olympic record Bob set stand?
4. Why do you think the judge decided not to send Bob to a detention center?
5. Why do you think Bob never knew his parents?

9 Benjamin Franklin

Benjamin Franklin had three distinct careers in his lifetime. He had success in the publishing business before he ever turned to science. He started working[25] as an apprentice in his brother's printing shop when he was only 12 years old. He loved to read. Once he tried to save money[50] for books by eating only vegetables. At age 23, he was publishing a newspaper. It was the first to use political cartoons. When he retired[75] from printing at age 39, he focused his interest in science. He invented the lightning rod and lightning bells while studying electricity. He was lucky[100] not to be killed during any of his experiments with lightning. Perhaps because he understood the relationship between electricity and fire, he started the first[125] fire insurance company in America. He finished his life as a statesman. He was appointed to the first Continental Congress. He was instrumental in drafting[150] the Declaration of Independence. At age 81, though quite frail, he signed the Constitution of the United States.[168]

1. What did Ben do before he turned to science?
2. What was his newspaper the first to do?
3. What two important documents did Ben sign?
4. Why would eating only vegetables help save money to buy books?
5. Why were Benjamin's experiments dangerous?

Amelia was ten years old when she first saw a plane, an unimpressive rusty heap at a state fair. Ten years later, however, she saw[25] a stunt-flying exhibition that changed her life. She had her first ride in an airplane in December of 1920. Within a week, she was taking[50] her first flying lesson. Within six months, she had saved enough money to buy her first plane, which she named Canary. In it, she set[75] her first women's record, flying at 14,000 feet. In 1928, flying with a co-pilot and a mechanic, she became the first woman to fly across[100] the Atlantic. A few years later, she made a solo flight across the Atlantic. Congress awarded her the Distinguished Flying Cross, the first ever given[125] to a woman. In 1937, she began a journey to be the first woman to fly around the world. The team had completed all but[150] 7,000 miles of the journey when it disappeared in the South Pacific. A massive rescue effort failed to turn up any clues concerning what happened,[175] and to this day, there are many theories about her fate.[186]

1. What was the first record set by Amelia?
2. What award was Amelia given for flying across the Atlantic?
3. How much of the round-the-world flight was left when Amelia disappeared?
4. How do we know Amelia was a woman who didn't waste time after making a decision?
5. Why couldn't the rescue teams find Amelia and her plane?

Cassius Clay

Cassius Clay was born in Louisville, Kentucky, and took up boxing only after someone stole his bicycle. Before he was known as Muhammad Ali, Cassius[25] was an Olympic gold medal winner at age eighteen. Four years later, he upset Sonny Liston to become world heavyweight champion. He then adopted the[50] Muslim faith and changed his name to Muhammad Ali. He successfully defended his title nine times and was well-known for his self-confidence and boastful statements.[75] Though he declared himself the "greatest of all time," few would argue with his assessment. When he refused to be inducted into the armed services,[100] he was stripped of his title and prevented from fighting for four years, when he was in his prime. Finally, the Supreme Court upheld his[125] appeal on religious grounds and he returned to the ring. His lifetime record was 56 wins and only 5 defeats. He was the only man[150] to win the heavyweight crown three times. He is as well-known in retirement as he was during his career. He suffers from Parkinson's disease, thought[175] to be caused by the many blows to his head.[185]

1. Why did Cassius change his name?
2. Why did Cassius take up boxing?
3. Where was Cassius born?
4. Why did Muhammad Ali refuse to join the armed services?
5. How did standing up for what he believed in hurt his career?

2 Jim Thorpe

● ●

Some consider Jim Thorpe the greatest all-around athlete of all time. He competed at the Olympics in Stockholm in 1912. He not only won the[25] decathlon and pentathlon, but he also destroyed the competition. He won nine of the fifteen separate track and field events that make up those two[50] competitions, and he did so by huge margins of victory. Thorpe was a member of the Sac and Fox Indian tribe. Before and after the[75] Olympics, he was a track and football star for Coach Pop Warner at the Carlisle Institute, a school for Native Americans. A year after winning[100] his gold medals, he was stripped of the medals when it was discovered that he had played for a minor league baseball team. Many athletes[125] at the time did this but used assumed names. Jim was honest and admitted that he did, and it cost him his medals. It was[150] not until thirty years after his death that he was given back his standing as an Olympic gold medalist.[169]

1. To which Native American tribe did Jim Thorpe belong?
2. Who was his coach in football?
3. Where did he compete in the Olympics?
4. Why did some consider Jim to be the best all-around athlete?
5. Why did other Olympic athletes use assumed names to play professional sports?

• •

Oscar didn't plan to be a boxer, though it shouldn't have come as a surprise because boxing had been in his family for generations. Oscar's[25] father and grandfather were boxers. Oscar's older brother is probably responsible for turning Oscar into a boxer. He first put boxing gloves on Oscar and[50] took him to the gym to learn to defend himself. When Oscar started winning fights, his relatives gave him small amounts of money as a[75] reward, and this prompted Oscar to keep fighting. His first real test would be the 1992 Olympics. When he left for Spain, he promised his[100] mother, who was ill, that he would return with the gold medal. In the gold medal bout, Oscar had to face a fighter who had[125] defeated him a year earlier. Oscar used his powerful left hand to knock down his opponent in the third round, and the referee stopped the[150] fight and declared him the winner. Oscar celebrated by dancing around the ring with a flag in each hand: one for Mexico and one for[175] the United States. Winning the gold was an emotional moment for Oscar, knowing that his mother was watching.[193]

1. Who else in Oscar's family had been boxers?
2. What did Oscar's relatives give him when he started winning fights?
3. Where were the Olympics held the year Oscar competed?
4. Why would the referee stop the fight after only three rounds?
5. Why do you think Oscar held two different flags when he won?

●●●

Wilma Rudolph's incredible accomplishment of being the first American woman to win three gold medals in the Olympics is more remarkable knowing what Wilma had[25] to overcome. She was born during the Great Depression to a poor family in Tennessee, the 20th of 22 children! She was born prematurely and[50] weighed less than five pounds. However, she could not be treated at the segregated hospital in town. As a child, she had one illness after[75] another, from mumps, scarlet fever, and chickenpox to double pneumonia. Then she was told she had polio and that she would never walk again. Her[100] mother, a determined woman, drove her 50 miles away for treatment to the black medical college of Fisk University in Nashville. She did this for[125] two years, until Wilma was able to walk with the aid of a metal leg brace. By the time Wilma was 12, she could walk[150] normally. It was then that she decided to become an athlete. In high school, she was a basketball star before going to college and becoming[175] a track star. She competed in her first Olympic games when she was 16 years old.[191]

1. How many children were in Wilma's family?
2. What sport did Wilma play first?
3. How far did Wilma's mother have to take her for therapy for her leg?
4. Why couldn't Wilma be treated at the hospital in town?
5. Why do you think Wilma was such a sick child?

5 Dan Gable

• •

It has been written that Dan is as well-known in wrestling for his coaching ability as he is for his own talents as a wrestler.[25] He coached the University of Iowa to 15 national championships in 21 years. He had attended Iowa State and while there compiled an impressive record,[50] winning his first 117 matches! He was voted All American three times and was upset only once, in his senior year at the NCAA final,[75] by a competitor who had dropped weight to compete in Dan's class. Dan has said that the loss, though devastating at the time, helped prepare[100] him for the Olympics two years later. He didn't let his opponents score a single point in the six matches leading toward his gold medal[125] win. Dan did not choose wrestling as his first sport. He first played football and baseball, ran track, and even swam. He found that he[150] liked wrestling better because there were no breaks and he could maintain his concentration.[164]

1. Where did Dan go to college?
2. Where did Dan coach?
3. How many losses did Dan have during his college career as a wrestler?
4. Why would someone drop weight in order to compete at a lower class?
5. What does Dan mean when he says that wrestling has no breaks?

6 Peggy Fleming

● ●

Peggy is credited with the revival of figure skating in the United States after a tragic accident. In 1961, when Peggy was only 11 years[25] old, the entire United States Figure Skating team was killed in a plane crash on its way to the world championships. Those who died in[50] the crash included Peggy's skating coach and most of her role models. For a while after the tragedy, Peggy didn't even feel like skating. However,[75] she was determined to be a champion and proved herself to be one many times over. She won five U.S. titles and three World titles[100] leading up to the 1968 Olympics. This was the first time the Olympics were broadcast live and in color. The graceful young skater in the[125] green dress captivated those watching. Peggy won the gold medal by an incredible 88 points over the silver medalist. Peggy's was the only gold medal[150] the U.S. team won that year at the Winter Games. Peggy went on to star in many television specials about skating, bringing the sport to[175] the forefront. Four different White House administrations invited her to visit. In 1980, she became the first skater invited to perform there.[197]

1. What tragedy happened when Peggy was 11 years old?
2. What was unique about the TV broadcast of the 1968 Olympics?
3. How many gold medals did the U.S. win at the Olympics that year?
4. What do you think Peggy's favorite color might be?
5. What made Peggy decide to keep skating after her coach was killed?

• •

Like some other talented athletes, Mark Spitz was not known for being modest. When he went to his first Olympic competition in 1968, he had[25] already set ten world records. He bragged that he would return from the Mexico City Olympics with six gold medals. When he won only two[50] events, both individual freestyles, he was disappointed. He went to Indiana University to train with the man who had coached him in the Olympics. He[75] accumulated numerous awards over the next four years, including eight individual NCAA titles. In 1971, he was named the country's top amateur athlete. He was[100] named World Swimmer of the Year in three of his four years during college. All of this training and competition left Mark feeling ready for[125] the Olympics in Munich. This time, he lived up to his own high expectations. He won four individual events and participated on three relay events,[150] which also resulted in gold medals. World records were set in each of those seven events.   Every newspaper and magazine report on the Olympics showed[175] pictures of Mark with seven gold medals around his neck. To this day, he is considered the fastest swimmer and is the first athlete to[200] win seven gold medals in one Olympiad.[207]

1. What city hosted the first Olympics in which Mark competed?
2. Where did Mark go to college?
3. Why did he choose that college?
4. Why are good athletes often not modest?
5. Why was he disappointed with two gold medals in his first Olympics?

8 Shirley Strickland

Shirley Strickland, a native of Australia, still holds the record for total amount of Olympic medals won by any female athlete. This accomplishment is even[25] more remarkable considering that female athletes at that time did not have as many events in which to compete. Shirley stated that she operated on[50] 90% enthusiasm and 10% technique. She represented her country in three Olympic Games. Her events were sprints, hurdles, and relays. She won eight[75] Olympic medals—three gold, one silver, and four bronze. In her career, she also set eight Olympic records. She was the first woman to ever[100] defend an Olympic athletics championship. She is still the only female to successfully defend an Olympic hurdles title. After her Olympic career, she became active[125] in politics in Australia. She also spoke out for environmental groups. She angered some in 2001 when she auctioned off her Olympic memorabilia. She asserted[150] that she had the right to do so. She wanted to help pay for her grandchildren's education. She also used the money to help buy[175] forests so the land could not be developed.[183]

1. In what Olympic events did Shirley compete?
2. In how many Olympic games did Shirley compete?
3. How many Olympic medals did Shirley win?
4. What did Shirley mean when she said she operated on 90% enthusiasm and 10% technique?
5. Why did some people become angry when Shirley sold her Olympic memorabilia?

9   Jesse Owens

Though the world knows him as Jesse, James Cleveland Owens was his given name, and his family called him J.C. When J.C. was eight, his[25] parents moved the family from their small town in Alabama to Cleveland, Ohio. On J.C.'s first day at his new school when his teacher asked[50] his name, she misunderstood and thought she heard Jesse instead of J.C. In high school, Jesse had to work part-time jobs after school which made[75] it difficult to train with the track team. After high school, Jesse enrolled at Ohio State University and joined the track team, but he couldn't[100] always stay in the same hotels or eat in the same restaurants as his teammates. At the Big Ten meet in 1935, Jesse did something[125] that no one had done before. He set three world records and tied a fourth. At the end of his sophomore year, Jesse was chosen[150] to compete in the 1936 Olympics to be held in Nazi Germany. Hitler was determined to use the Olympics to prove to the world that[175] the "Aryan" people were the dominant race. Jesse clearly demonstrated to the world the ignorance of that belief. He won four gold medals—three individual[200] and one team—and set Olympic records in all but one of the events. He became the first American in the history of Olympic Track[225] and Field to win four gold medals in a single Olympics.[236]

1. How did J.C. end up being called Jesse?
2. Where did Jesse attend college?
3. Where were the 1936 Olympics held?
4. Why do you think Jesse had to work part-time jobs after school?
5. Why couldn't Jesse stay in the same hotels as his college teammates?

10 Scott Hamilton

• •

One of the most famous male figure skaters, Scott Hamilton has faced adversity after adversity. Scott was adopted when he was six weeks old, and[25] his first major challenge occurred when he was two years old. He contracted an illness that made him stop growing. His puzzled doctors tried various[50] treatments, most of them unsuccessful. It is thought that Scott's intensive exercise was responsible for restarting his growth. He took skating lessons as well as[75] played ice hockey. As an adult, Scott has survived cancer, due in part to the same positive attitude and determination that helped him become an[100] award-winning skater. He has recently recovered from a benign brain tumor. Despite the medical challenges he has faced, Scott has excelled at all of his[125] endeavors. His awards and titles are numerous and impressive. He won 16 consecutive championships. He was inducted into the United States Olympic Hall of Fame[150] and the Madison Square Garden Walk of Fame. He is considered an articulate sports analyst. He has also written a well-received autobiography and is a[175] motivational speaker.[177]

1. How old was Scott when he was adopted?
2. How many consecutive championships has Scott won?
3. What was one of the medical problems Scott encountered?
4. What might have happened when Scott was little if he hadn't taken up skating?
5. What does a positive attitude have to do with beating an illness?

Methods used to grade passages in this book

Fully recognizing the shortcomings of any of the methodology used to determine a passage's readability, I made the following decisions when writing the passages for this book:

▶ I used the Spache Formula to determine the readability of the passages for grades 1 through 4 (Levels A through D). It didn't seem logical to use a method that didn't take vocabulary into account. Even if the vocabulary reference list is outdated, it shouldn't affect these passages as it would a textbook since I purposely avoided writing about "current" topics, such as computers, digital audio players, and cell phones.

▶ I used the Flesch-Kincaid Grade Level formula (from Microsoft® Office Word 2003 SP2) to analyze the passages for grades 5 through 8 (Levels E through H).

▶ I also used the Dale-Chall formula on the fifth-grade passages (Level E) to yield information about vocabulary words that might be difficult for the student. In Appendix B on pages 135-142, *Instructor's Guide to the Passages*, I noted any words in the passage that are not on the Dale-Chall list (words that should be familiar to 80% of fourth graders). You might want to review those words with the student before the baseline reading to increase accuracy. You might also put the words on flashcards for extra practice; however, word identification drills are most useful when you use words the student missed rather than an arbitrarily assigned group of words.

How the passages are organized

I used a letter system to indicate the levels of the passages so that a student wouldn't be discouraged if he were reading at a level lower than his grade level. For example, if a student notes that he is reading a Level 3 passage, he is likely to know that it is a third-grade passage. Conversely, he is less likely to determine that Level C corresponds to a third-grade passage. I have provided specifics about grade levels in the *Instructor's Guide to the Passages* on pages 135-142.

In addition, I arranged the non-sequential stories within each grade level in order of increasing difficulty according to the formula I used to grade the passages. There are often instances in which multiple passages are at the same level (e.g., 7.3).

Content of stories

Passages for grades 1 through 3 (Levels A, B, and C) are about fictional characters. This is true of the sequential and the non-sequential passages. I did this to avoid "hard" names of real characters and also to maintain the student's interest. Passages for grades 4 through 8 (Levels D through H) are fact-based.

When using the sequential passages (provided only for Levels A, B, and C), you may need to remind the student about the characters or what happened in the last passage he read. Fact-based stories lend themselves to further comprehension activities. In fact, I have provided notes with additional information about the content for some of the levels. You'll find these notes in the *Instructor's Guide to the Passages* on pages 135-142.

Comprehension

It's important that students know they are reading for comprehension. I've included five comprehension questions for each passage in this book. The first three questions require the student to recall factual information that he can easily find in the text. The last two questions require the student to draw a conclusion or infer the information. You can have the student answer these questions after the baseline reading or after completing the multiple readings of the passage.

Length of Passages

In general, I chose the length of the passages based on what a reader at the 50th to 70th percentile of reading rate could complete in one minute. This means that the students you're working with (almost certainly below the 50th percentile) will take more than a minute. This will allow you to use either the Count Up or the Count Down method. If you're using the Count Down method, you need a passage the student won't finish before the minute runs out. Some of the sequential passages (grades 1-3, Levels A-C) may be longer to allow for development of the storyline.

Word Count

There are many ways automatic word counts are calculated depending on the source you use. Most word count tools on your word processor count words differently. The following are some examples of different ways the word count of a passage is calculated:

▶ count the characters in an average line, divide by six, count the number of lines in the passage, and multiply these two numbers together

▶ assume that there are 250 words per page and estimate the amount in the passage as compared to the entire page

▶ physically count each word

▶ count the number of characters and divide by five or six for a word count with words of average length

Due to the varying possibilities, I physically counted the words in each passage in this book to determine its word count. Numbers indicating the word counts are included as superscript numbers within the passages (in 25-word increments). When using the Count Down method, this will make it easier to calculate the total number of words a student has read when his time is up. Note that I did not include the titles when determining the word counts of the passages. The total number of words in each passage is also included in the *Instructor's Guide to the Passages* on pages 135-142.

Calculating words correct per minute (WCPM)

To calculate words correct per minute, see the formulae in Appendix Q, page 157. To make this task easier, I've included a superscript number after every 25 words in each passage and at the end of the passage for the total number of words. These numbers do not include the words in the title.

Rate

How fast should the student read? Pinnell et al. (1995) determined that students need to read 130 words correct per minute (WCPM) to be proficient on assessments at grade four. After computing a student's WCPM (see Appendix Q, page 157), compare his rate against the normative data in Appendices R and S on pages 158 and 159.

Selecting passages for the student to read

Before selecting passages to use for repeat reading (or other practice materials for increasing attention to the text), refer to the information in Chapter 4 on readability formulae. Select a passage that is at the independent or instructional level for that student. A student reading at the independent level should miss no more than 5% of the text on his first read through (baseline). If the student needs to build confidence in his reading skills, you may want to have him start with this level. A student reading at the instructional level is 90-94% accurate on the passage on baseline reading. The *Instructor's Guide to the Passages* on pages 135-142 includes information for each passage that indicates the number of words a student can miss to be at the independent or instructional levels. When a student completes all of the passages at a grade level, move him to the next level of passages, keeping in mind the information about independent and instructional reading levels.

Independent Level

For the student to be at the independent level (95-100% accurate), he must miss fewer than 6% of the words on the baseline reading. To figure out how many words that is, follow this example using passage 10 in Level D, *Uncle George Visits*, which has 186 words:

$$186 \times 94\% = 174.8$$
$$186 - 175 = 11$$
11 words = 6% of the words in the passage

To be at the independent level for this passage, the student must have fewer than 11 errors (i.e., 0-10 errors) on his baseline reading. If he misses 11 or more words, try using a different passage from the same level or from a lower level.

Instructional Level

For the student to be at the instructional level (between 90% and 94% accurate), he will miss at least 6% of the words but fewer than 11% of the words on the baseline reading. To figure out how many words that is, follow this example using passage 10 in Level D, *Uncle George Visits*, which has 186 words:

11 words = 6% of the words in the passage (see Independent Level)
$$186 \times 89\% = 165.5$$
$$186 - 166 = 20$$
20 words = 11% of the words in the passage

To be at the instructional level for this passage, the student will have 11-19 errors on his baseline reading. If he misses fewer than 11 words, try using a different passage from the same level or from a higher level. If he misses 20 or more words, try using a different passage, preferably from a lower level.

Before reading a passage

Look over the passage to determine any words the student may find difficult. For example, characters' names that are unfamiliar to the student may be challenging. Although for the Level E (grade 5) passages, I noted any words that are not on the Dale-Chall list (words that should be familiar to 80% of fourth graders), it's important to identify words that are hard for each particular student.

Other uses for the reading passages

You can use these passages for one-on-one, oral, assisted repeat readings. Kuhn and Stahl (2003) have reviewed different ways in which reading passages can be used to improve fluency.

▶ Have the student independently practice reading the passage multiple times, either silently or orally. Establish a words-per-minute goal for the student, and have him read the passage until he reaches the goal.

▶ Instead of giving the student a words-per-minute goal, have him read the passage a set number of times (typically three or four times).

▶ Tape-record yourself or someone reading the passage at the desired rate and with good prosody, and have the student read along with the tape recording (Hollingsworth, 1970).

▶ Using the tape recording you made, have the student listen to the passage several times, silently "reading along." When the student thinks he is ready to read the passage fluently, have him read it to you (Chomsky, 1978; Carbo, 1981). In this way, the student knows that at some point he has to read the passage aloud to you. This is important because simply listening to stories doesn't seem to have an effect on reading achievement (Evans & Carr, 1985; Leinhardt et al., 1981).

▶ Have the student read to another student who is a good reader (and possibly from an older grade).

Instructor's guide to the passages

This guide includes the following information:

▶ grade level of story (A, B, C, etc.)

▶ indication of sequential or non-sequential (Levels A, B, and C only)

▶ number of words in the passage

▶ number of words the student can miss on baseline reading and be at independent or instructional levels

▶ Flesch-Kincaid Grade Level and Flesch Reading Ease (shaded for Levels A-D since they are reference numbers only and were not used to level those passages)

▶ Spache rating for Levels A-D only

▶ Dale-Chall rating for Levels E-H (shaded since it is a reference number only and was not used to level those passages)

▶ additional notes for some levels to prompt further discussion

▶ vocabulary words determined to be difficult by a Dale-Chall analysis (Level E only)

▶ references used to gather factual information for passages in Levels D-H

Note: Shaded regions are for reference use only.

Level and Grade	Passage	Words in passage (not including the title)	Independent level (# of errors)	Instructional level (# of errors)	Flesch-Kincaid	Flesch Reading Ease	Spache
Level A — Grade 1 Sequential	1. Mac and Bell Dig a Hole	100	0-5	6-10	0.2	100	1.8
	2. Mac Gets Stuck	94	0-5	6-9	1.1	100	1.9
	3. Mac and Bell Are Rescued	100	0-5	6-10	0.0	100	1.7
	4. Bobby's New Pool	93	0-5	6-9	0.1	100	1.9
	5. Mac and Bell Learn to Climb	70	0-3	4-7	0.0	100	1.8
	6. Mac and Bell Go for a Swim	100	0-5	6-10	0.0	100	1.9
	7. Mac Takes Bell's Toy	91	0-4	5-9	0.0	100	1.9
	8. Mac Hides the Toy Frog	94	0-5	6-9	0.0	100	1.8
	9. Bell Misses His Toy	95	0-5	6-9	0.0	100	1.8
	10. Bobby Comes to the Rescue	103	0-5	6-10	1.1	100	1.7
Level A — Grade 1 Non-sequential	1. The Cat and the Dog	48	0-2	3-4	0.0	100	1.2
	2. Pete Cannot Sleep	48	0-2	3-4	0.0	100	1.5
	3. The Kite	52	0-2	3-5	0.0	100	1.6
	4. Ruff Goes for a Ride	53	0-2	3-5	0.0	100	1.6
	5. The Hot Day	48	0-2	3-4	0.0	100	1.7
	6. Jan Makes Up a Game	53	0-2	3-5	0.0	100	1.7
	7. The Lost Hat	53	0-2	3-5	0.0	100	1.7
	8. Ben Can Jump	80	0-4	5-8	0.0	100	1.7
	9. The New Bike	65	0-3	4-6	0.0	100	1.8
	10. Mike Can Draw	64	0-3	4-6	0.0	100	1.8

Note: Shaded regions are for reference use only.

Level and Grade	Passage	Words in passage (not including the title)	Independent level (# of errors)	Instructional level (# of errors)	Flesch-Kincaid	Flesch Reading Ease	Spache
Level B — Grade 2 Sequential	1. Beth Helps Jed	101	0-5	6-10	2.1	97.7	2.6
	2. Jed Kicks Too Hard	107	0-5	6-11	1.1	100	2.1
	3. Jed Has an Idea	105	0-5	6-11	0.9	100	2.4
	4. Buster is Missing	94	0-5	6-9	1.3	98.9	2.3
	5. Buster and Spike	102	0-5	6-10	1.8	97.0	2.1
	6. Game Night for Beth	105	0-5	6-11	2.2	97.8	2.7
	7. Beth Scores	106	0-5	6-11	2.8	91.7	2.8
	8. The Celebration	94	0-5	6-9	2.7	89.2	2.9
	9. Jed Joins a Team	98	0-5	6-10	1.6	97.6	2.8
	10. Jed's First Game	110	0-6	7-11	1.9	99.1	2.5
Level B — Grade 2 Non-sequential	1. Josh Finds a Bug	45	0-2	3-4	0.0	100	2.0
	2. Muffy Climbs a Tree	60	0-3	4-6	0.0	100	2.0
	3. Snake in the Grass	65	0-3	4-6	2.2	93.1	2.0
	4. Sam Bakes a Cake	50	0-2	3-5	0.0	100	2.1
	5. Steve and Mom Bake	59	0-3	4-6	1.0	100	2.5
	6. The Magic Jacket	67	0-3	4-6	3.9	83.4	2.7
	7. The New Coach	62	0-3	4-6	2.5	95.3	2.7
	8. Drew's First Solo Flight	69	0-3	4-7	2.5	97	2.8
	9. Disney World	80	0-4	5-8	4.2	85.4	2.9
	10. The Shopping Trip	70	0-3	4-7	1.8	98.6	2.9

Note: Shaded regions are for reference use only.

Level and Grade	Passage	Words in passage (not including the title)	Independent level (# of errors)	Instructional level (# of errors)	Flesch-Kincaid	Flesch Reading Ease	Spache
Level C — Grade 3 Sequential	1. The Walled City	133	0-7	8-14	5.1	82.0	3.3
	2. Lucas and His Family	140	0-7	8-14	5.3	72.4	3.1
	3. Lucas's Secret Missions	141	0-7	8-15	5.2	85.3	3.4
	4. The Guards	137	0-7	8-14	5.6	78.6	3.7
	5. Lucas Watches the Guards	171	0-9	10-18	5.3	84.6	3.6
	6. Lucas Starts His Patrol	174	0-9	10-18	5.3	84.7	3.4
	7. Lucas Circles the City	140	0-7	8-14	5.6	79.6	3.1
	8. Lucas Gets a Surprise	176	0-10	11-18	5.5	77.7	3.2
	9. Lucas and Carlotta Spot a Problem	133	0-7	8-14	5.4	79.4	3.3
	10. Lucas and Carlotta Alert the Guards	144	0-8	9-15	5.4	78.9	3.7
Level C — Grade 3 Non-sequential	1. Smoky Mountains	134	0-7	8-14	5.1	84.3	3.1
	2. Shadows on the Wall	149	0-8	9-15	6.6	77.1	3.1
	3. The New Kid	119	0-6	7-12	4.0	92.2	3.2
	4. The Birthday Party	121	0-6	7-12	6.7	70.8	3.2
	5. The Lost Money	139	0-7	8-14	4.3	91.3	3.2
	6. Going Camping	136	0-7	8-14	5.1	85.1	3.3
	7. The New Pet	137	0-7	8-14	6.2	80.7	3.4
	8. Homework, Homework, Homework	133	0-7	8-14	5.2	78.7	3.5
	9. Janet's Special Box	128	0-7	8-13	6.3	78.2	3.7
	10. The Woods	146	0-8	9-15	5.4	88.6	3.8

Note: Shaded regions are for reference use only.

Level and Grade	Passage	Words in passage (not including the title)	Independent level (# of errors)	Instructional level (# of errors)	Flesch-Kincaid	Flesch Reading Ease	Spache	Notes for Further Discussion
Level D — Grade 4	1. Ann's Mother Gets to Vote	165	0-9	10-17	8.2	68.2	4.0	Wyoming was the first state, in 1869, to give women the right to vote and to allow them to run for office. In fact, it also had the first woman governor in 1929.
	2. Tom Goes to a Tea Party	193	0-11	12-20	6.9	79.8	4.0	To protect a tax placed on American settlers by the British government, a group of men who called themselves the Sons of Liberty, boarded an English ship in 1773 and threw the cargo overboard. They dressed as Indians to disguise themselves.
	3. Susan Meets Stevie	192	0-11	12-20	9.1	63.9	4.0	Steveland Judkins Morris (Stevie Wonder) was born blind in Michigan. He had his own recording contract by the time he was 13.
	4. Russ Helps the Family Pack	184	0-10	11-19	7.9	74.3	4.1	Farmers in Oklahoma were driven off their land by the great dust bowl—a combination of wind and drought. They moved across America looking for work, but the depression was going on and it made the search difficult.
	5. Liz Dreams Big	189	0-10	11-20	8.7	66.4	4.1	Elizabeth Blackwell, the first American woman to become a doctor, studied privately because no school would accept her. Finally, Geneva Medical School in western NY enrolled her. She graduated in the top of her class in 1849.
	6. Bad Boy Bonney	209	0-12	13-22	8.7	73.5	4.2	William Bonney, known as Billy the Kid, was born in New York but moved to New Mexico when he was young. When grown, he led a band of outlaws. He escaped from jail while awaiting execution and was killed by Pat Garrett.
	7. Maria's Neighbor Is a Pioneer	160	0-9	10-17	8.6	68.6	4.2	In 1986, Christa McAuliffe, a high school teacher, was chosen to be the first teacher to go into outer space. The shuttle, *Challenger*, exploded on takeoff and killed her and the 6 astronauts on board.
	8. Amy's Neighbors	179	0-10	11-19	8.5	68.9	4.2	The Wright brothers, Orville and Wilbur, were leaders in the aviation field. Their first man-powered flight took place in 1903 in North Carolina. They took their plane there to fly it because of the wide-open spaces.
	9. Rosa Goes to School	162	0-9	10-17	8.7	73.6	4.2	Rosa Parks grew up in rural Alabama (Montgomery). As an adult, she was famous for starting the Civil Rights Movement in 1955 when she refused to move to the back of the bus.
	10. Uncle George Visits	186	0-10	11-19	9.5	63.5	4.3	Gold prospectors went to South Dakota in 1874 and encountered hostile Sioux. General Custer was part of the force sent to protect the prospectors. In 1876, he defied orders and led his troops into an ambush. He and his 200 soldiers were all killed.

Note: Shaded region is for reference use only.

Level and Grade	Passage	Words in passage (not including the title)	Independent level (# of errors)	Instructional level (# of errors)	Flesch-Kincaid	Flesch Reading Ease	Dale-Chall	Difficult Words (according to the Dale-Chall analysis)		
Level E — Grade 5 (Weather & Natural Disasters)	1. Floods	148	0-8	9-15	5.7	79.9	5.7	absorbed evaporates occur imbalance saturated	basic types regular dangerous scientists	predicting Doppler Radar
	2. Wildfires	158	0-8	9-16	5.1	81.5	6.2	areas often occur purpose arson	prone main trench helicopters	
	3. Ice Storms	135	0-7	8-14	5.2	79.0	5.1	temperatures glisten crackling	property injure restore	
	4. Earthquakes	143	0-8	9-15	5.3	75.1	7.1	unlike disasters related occur California Nevada	risk area Midwest Mississippi prone quake	shocks severity measured severe objects
	5. Drought	142	0-8	9-15	5.4	76.8	7.4	drought simply lack occurs predicted period	affected irrigation system effects tractor severe	shortage
	6. Lightning	146	0-8	9-15	5.5	78.6	4.6	strike protection safe		
	7. Hail Storms	162	0-9	10-17	5.6	80.6	5.9	usually occurs super layers rotating recycling	per extremely Nebraska diameter crater serious	
	8. Blizzards	134	0-7	8-14	5.7	75.7	6.0	blizzard extremely considered difficult factor	per temperature zero degrees tissue	
	9. Hurricanes	152	0-8	9-16	5.8	74.1	4.9	hurricanes national female rotated retired	Katrina levees surrounding Orleans	
	10. Tornadoes	144	0-8	9-15	5.9	73.6	6.0	tornadoes area Texas Dakotas type super per	funnel scientists special rank severity range zero	

Note: Shaded region is for reference use only.

Level and Grade	Passage	Words in passage (not including the title)	Independent level (# of errors)	Instructional level (# of errors)	Flesch-Kincaid	Flesch Reading Ease	Dale-Chall	Notes for Further Discussion
Level F — Grade 6 (U.S. First Ladies)	1. Martha Dandridge Custis Washington	161	0-9	10-17	6.3	67.3	7.3	George Washington in office 1789-1897 Martha born 1731; died 1802
	2. Edith Kermit Carow Roosevelt	157	0-8	9-16	6.5	68.2	7.6	Theodore Roosevelt in office 1901-1909 Edith born 1861; died 1948
	3. Frances Folsom Cleveland	167	0-9	10-17	6.6	72.1	6.3	Grover Cleveland in office 1885-1889 and 1893-1897 Frances born 1864; died 1947
	4. Jacqueline Lee Bouvier Kennedy	158	0-8	9-16	6.6	69.2	6.3	John F. Kennedy in office 1961-1963 Jacqueline born 1929; died 1994
	5. Hillary Rodham Clinton	159	0-9	10-16	6.7	66.5	6.8	Bill Clinton in office 1993-2001 Hillary born 1947
	6. Julia Dent Grant	167	0-9	10-17	6.7	67.5	6.7	Ulysses S. Grant in office 1869-1877 Julia born 1826; died 1902
	7. Dolley Payne Todd Madison	170	0-9	10-18	6.8	66.4	7.1	James Madison in office 1809-1817 Dolley born 1766; died 1849
	8. Lou Henry Hoover	172	0-9	10-18	6.8	66.3	7.2	Herbert Hoover in office 1929-1933 Lou born 1874; died 1944
	9. Rosalynn Smith Carter	162	0-9	10-17	6.8	63.9	7.1	Jimmy Carter in office 1977-1981 Rosalynn born 1927
	10. Claudia Taylor "Lady Bird" Johnson	173	0-9	10-18	6.9	67.1	6.6	Lyndon B. Johnson in office 1963-1969 Claudia born 1912
Level G — Grade 7 (Success Stories)	1. Alan Simpson	169	0-9	10-18	7.2	64.4	7.7	
	2. Paul Orfalea	197	0-11	12-21	7.2	71.9	5.1	
	3. Jewel	192	0-11	12-20	7.3	71.1	6.6	
	4. Nancy Lopez	173	0-9	10-18	7.3	72.8	6.7	
	5. Gloria Steinem	160	0-9	10-17	7.5	60.5	7.0	
	6. Richard Branson	167	0-9	10-17	7.5	67.8	6.6	
	7. Oprah Winfrey	178	0-10	11-19	7.5	67.2	6.4	
	8. Bob Beamon	182	0-10	11-19	7.8	68.2	6.0	
	9. Benjamin Franklin	168	0-9	10-17	7.8	58.4	6.6	
	10. Amelia Earhart	186	0-10	11-19	7.9	66.0	6.5	

Note: Shaded region is for reference use only.

Level and Grade	Passage	Words in passage (not including the title)	Independent level (# of errors)	Instructional level (# of errors)	Flesch-Kincaide	Flesch Reading Ease	Dale-Chall	Notes
Level H — Grade 8 (Sports Heroes)	1. Cassius Clay	185	0-10	11-19	8.0	65.1	7.4	DOB 1/17/42 From Kentucky Competed on 1976 U.S. Olympic Team
	2. Jim Thorpe	169	0-9	10-18	8.1	67.0	7.5	5/28/1887 to 3/28/1953 From Oklahoma Competed on 1912 U.S. Olympic Team
	3. Oscar De La Hoya	193	0-11	12-20	8.2	67.1	6.5	DOB 2/4/73 From California Competed on 1992 U.S. Olympic Team
	4. Wilma Rudolph	191	0-10	11-20	8.4	63.2	7.0	6/23/40 to 1/12/94 From Tennessee Competed on 1956 & 1960 U.S. Olympic Teams
	5. Dan Gable	164	0-9	10-17	8.5	66.0	7.3	DOB 10/25/48 From Canada Competed on 1972 U.S. Olympic Team
	6. Peggy Fleming	197	0-11	12-21	8.5	60.3	6.6	DOB 7/27/48 From California Competed on 1964 & 1968 U.S. Olympic Teams
	7. Mark Spitz	207	0-11	12-22	8.6	59.4	7.6	DOB 2/10/50 From California Competed on 1968 & 1972 U.S. Olympic Teams
	8. Shirley Strickland	183	0-10	11-19	8.6	54.3	8.0	7/18/25 to 2/11/04 From Australia Competed on Australian Olympic Team in 1948, 1952, 1956, 1968, 1976
	9. Jesse Owens	236	0-13	14-25	8.7	67.1	7.4	9/12/13 to 3/31/80 From Alabama Competed on 1936 U.S. Olympic Team
	10. Scott Hamilton	177	0-10	11-18	8.8	54.4	8.9	DOB 8/28/58 From Ohio Competed on 1980 & 1984 U.S. Olympic Teams

I obtained factual information for some of the passages from the following sources:

Level D

Levy, P. (2000). *The 50 States: Over 100 questions and answers to things you want to know.* Bournemouth, Dorset, UK: Paragon Publishing.

Level E

1 www.pbs.org/newshour/infocus/floods/science.html
2 www.fema.gov/kids/wldfire.htm
3 www.nws.noaa.gov/om/brochures/wntrstm.htm
4 www.fema.gov/kids/quake.htm
5 www.drought.unl.edu/kids/whatis.htm
6 www.skydiary.com/kids/lightning.html
7 www.skydiary.com/kids/tornadoes.html
   www.ggweather.com/archive/weacorneraug12.htm
8 www.ussartf.org/blizzards.htm
9 www.en.wikipedia.org/wiki/Hurricane_Katrina
10 www.skydiary.com/kids/tornadoes.html

Level G

1 www.cjcj.org/pdf/secondchances.pdf
2 www.schwablearning.org/on_the_web.asp?siteid=www.ldonline.org/first_person/orfalea.html
3 www.schwablearning.org/on_the_web.asp?siteid=www.girlslife.com/jewel.html
4 www.latinosportslegends.com/2001/lopez_nancy_battle_against_strokes_heartdisease-701.htm
   www.latinosportslegends.com/Lopez_Nancy-bio.htm
5 www.npr.org/templates/story/story.php?storyId=4805246
   www.en.wikipedia.org/wiki/Gloria_Steinem
6 www.cjcj.org/pdf/secondchances.pdf
7 www.schwablearning.org/on the web.asp?siteid=www.johnshepler.com/articles/branson.html
   %20&popref=%3A//www.schwablearning.org/articles.asp%3Fr%3D258
8 www.woopidoo.com/biography/oprah-winfrey.htm
9 www.ameliaearhart.com/about/biography2.html
10 www.school-for-champions.com/biographies/franklin.htm

Level H

1 www.infoplease.com/ce6/people/A0803335.html
2 www.en.wikipedia.org/wiki/Dan Gable
   Zavoral, N. (2003). *A season on the mat: Dan Gable and the pursuit of perfection.* New York: Simon & Schuster.
3 www.lkwdpl.org/wihohio/rudo-wil.htm
4 www.infoplease.com/spot/mm-thorpe.html
5 www.latinosportslegends.com/Delahoya_Oscar_bio.htm
6 www.espn.go.com/sportscentury/features/00016480.html
7 www.peggyfleming.net/story.html
8 www.geocities.com/geetee/bios/shirl.html
9 www.jesseowens.com/jobio2.html
10 www.webmd.com/content/Biography/9/111238.htm

Name: _____

Date	Passage

All repeat reading is designed to:

▶ increase reading speed

▶ transfer that improvement in speed to subsequent material

▶ enhance comprehension with each successive reading of text

For all types of repeat reading, keep the following in mind:

▶ The student **must** run his finger under the line of text as he's reading to help his eyes follow along. Many students do not like to do this, but you should insist on it.

▶ For students who are very distractible, you may need to cover the remaining lines of text with a card or paper.

▶ Use materials that the student can read at the independent level (95-100% accuracy on first reading) or at the instructional level (90-94% accuracy on first reading). If the student has more errors than that, the passage is too difficult. The goal of this activity is not to work on decoding.

▶ Correct any errors the student makes by immediately saying the word correctly. You may ask the student to stop and repeat the word correctly, or you may let him go on reading. Some students become too frustrated when you ask them to repeat.

▶ It's important to count each error as it occurs. The easiest way to keep track of errors with repeat reading is to make two copies of the passage. As the student reads from one, you can use the other to note any errors. Write a small "B" above each error the student makes during baseline reading, a "1" above each error on the first reading after baseline, a "2" above each error on the second reading after baseline, etc. After the student completes the passage, you may want to highlight the errors on the student's copy.

▶ Have the student read the passage three or four times to get the most benefit.

▶ Record the student's accuracy as well as his rate.

▶ Use a visible measure of progress to motivate the student (See Appendices K-P, pages 151-156).

▶ Use different types of repeat reading practice for different students (See Appendices E-H, pages 145-148, for descriptions).

▶ Give the student 15 to 20 minutes of daily practice with repeat reading.

▶ Ask the student comprehension questions to remind him to pay attention to the content of what he reads.

This technique is best used with beginning readers who read accurately but slowly (less than 45 wpm); however, it has also been used with students in middle and high school who were reading at least three grade levels behind their grade level. In echo reading, you can use your finger to follow the line of text, as the student may not move his finger along quickly enough. There are two variations on this method—one uses baseline measures and one does not.

Using baseline timing

Have the student read the passage while you time the baseline reading. Use a highlighter to mark any errors. Determine if the passage is at the target level you selected (i.e., independent or instructional). Discuss any words the student missed. Then you and the student should read the passage in unison. After reading together several times, have the student read the passage on his own while you time him. Praise the student for the time he has taken off from the last reading as compared to the baseline reading (first reading). Discuss how the errors have decreased. Give the student a list of any words he consistently had difficulty with so he can practice them later. Point out to the student how much smoother the reading sounded as the rate increased.

Without baseline reading

Let the student help pick out the material he will read. Rarely will students pick something that is too difficult. Tell the student that you'll begin by reading the material in unison. When he is ready, he can tap you on the arm to indicate that he wants to read solo. When he makes an error, stop him and tell him the correct word. Then you and the student should reread that sentence together. You can then decide if you want the student to continue solo reading or if he should begin reading in unison with you again. This approach does not use repeat readings of the same passage, but you might adapt it and have the student read solo several times after achieving some fluency with the unison approach.

To assure comprehension of the passage, ask the student a few questions about the content. You want the student to know that just because he is working on increasing his speed, you are also concerned with how much he understood.

References: Dowhower, 1994; Heckelman, 1969, 1986; Mefford & Pettegrew, 1997; Topping, 1987; Topping & Whitley, 1990; Young et al., 1996

1. Have the student read the passage while you time the baseline reading. Use a highlighter to mark any errors. If the student makes too many errors (more than 5% for independent level or more than 10% for instructional level), choose another passage. Discuss any words the student missed.

2. After the baseline reading, tell the student to read the passage again, this time as quickly as he can. Let him know that you will correct him if he makes an error. During the reading, immediately correct any errors the student makes by saying what the word should have been. You can decide if you want the student to repeat the word correctly. If the student makes a major error, you can turn off the stopwatch to discuss what was wrong with the word and then continue the timed reading. It's important to count each error as it occurs. Use any method you choose to help you remember the total number of errors, such as making a mark on the corner of the passage or counting on your fingers. Another suggestion is to make two copies of the passage. As the student reads from one, you can use the other to note any errors. Write a small "B" above each error the student makes during baseline reading, a "I" for each error on the first reading after the baseline, etc. In this way, you can review all of the errors with the student.

3. At the end of the passage, tell the student his time and the number of errors. Ask him what his goal is for the next reading. How much faster does he think he can read and how many errors can he eliminate? Then reset the stopwatch and have the student read again. Follow the guidelines described above. At the end of the passage, record the student's time and number of errors. Have the student set time and error goals for the next reading and repeat.

4. Praise the student for the time he has taken off from the last reading as compared to the baseline reading (first reading). Discuss how the errors have decreased. Give the student a list of any words he consistently had difficulty with so he can practice them later. Point out to the student how much smoother the reading sounded as the rate increased.

5. To assure comprehension of the passage, ask the student a few questions about the content. You want the student to know that just because he is working on increasing his speed, you are also concerned with how much he understood.

References: Samuels, 1979, 1988; Samuels et al., 1992

1. Have the student read the passage while you time the baseline reading. Use a highlighter to mark any errors. If the student makes too many errors (more than 5% for independent level or 10% for instructional level), choose another passage. Write one error word on each index card. Complete a variety of activities to drill the student on recognition of the words.

    Activity 1   Turn the cards over quickly and have the student say them.

    Activity 2   Place all the cards facedown on the table and have the student turn one over and read it.

    Activity 3   Hold two cards facing you and randomly turn one to face the student for him to read. Then turn the other card to face the student. Repeat turning cards around, alternating between words. Sometimes turn the same card around two times in a row. When you are confident that the student recognizes these words, continue with the repeat reading.

2. After the baseline reading, tell the student to read the passage again, this time as quickly as he can. Let him know that if he makes an error, you will say the word correctly. You can decide if you want the student to repeat the word correctly before going on with reading. During the reading, if the student makes an error, immediately say what the word should have been. If the student makes a major error, you can turn off the stopwatch to discuss what was wrong with the word and then continue the timed reading. It's important to count each error as it occurs. Use any method you choose to help you remember the total number of errors, such as making a mark on the corner of the passage or counting on your fingers. Another suggestion is to make two copies of the passage. As the student reads from one, you can use the other to note any errors. Write a small "B" above each error the student makes during baseline reading, a "1" for each error on the first reading after the baseline, etc. In this way, you can review all of the errors with the student. If any of the words are "new" errors (those not identified on the baseline reading and drilled), make a card and add it to the ones you made previously. You can drill again between trials.

3. At the end of the passage, tell the student his time and the number of errors. Ask him what his goal is for the next reading. How much faster does he think he can read and how many errors can he eliminate? Then reset the stopwatch and have the student read again. Follow the guidelines described above. At the end of the passage, record the student's time and number of errors. Have the student set time and error goals for the next reading and repeat.

4. Praise the student for the time he has taken off from the last reading as compared to the baseline reading (first reading). Discuss how the errors have decreased. Give the student a list of any words he consistently had difficulty with so he can practice them later. Point out to the student how much smoother the reading sounded as the rate increased.

5. To assure comprehension of the passage, ask the student a few questions about the content. You want the student to know that just because he is working on increasing his speed, you are also concerned with how much he understood.

1. Have the student read the passage while you time the baseline reading. Use a highlighter to mark any errors. If the student makes too many errors (more than 5% for independent level or 10% for instructional level), choose another passage. Discuss any words the student missed. Highlight any areas you think would help the student to sound more fluent. You might mark all of the punctuation or just those that the student is ignoring. You might highlight a phrase or two and help the student practice reading/saying those phrases with meaning. You can even read the whole passage for the student, modeling good phrasing and expression.

2. After the baseline reading, tell the student to read the passage again, this time as quickly as he can. Let him know that if he makes an error, you will say the word correctly. You can decide if you want the student to repeat the word correctly before going on with reading. During the reading, if the student makes an error, immediately say what the word should have been. If the student makes a major error, you can turn off the stopwatch to discuss what was wrong with the word and then continue the timed reading. It's important to count each error as it occurs. Use any method you choose to help you remember the total number of errors, such as making a mark on the corner of the passage or counting on your fingers. Another suggestion is to make two copies of the passage. As the student reads from one, you can use the other to note any errors. Write a small "B" above each error the student makes during baseline reading, a "1" for each error on the first reading after the baseline, etc. In this way, you can review all of the errors with the student.

3. At the end of the passage, tell the student his time and the number of errors. Point out whether he attended to the syntactic and rhythmic cues you had discussed. Ask him what his goal is for the next reading. How much faster does he think he can read and how many errors can he eliminate? Then reset the stopwatch and have the student read again. Follow the guidelines described above. At the end of the passage, record the student's time and number of errors. Have the student set time and error goals for the next reading and repeat.

4. Praise the student for the time he has taken off from the last reading as compared to the baseline reading (first reading). Congratulate him on reading with more expression. Point out phrases or sentences that he read well with meaning. Discuss how the errors have decreased. Give the student a list of any words he consistently had difficulty with so he can practice them later. Point out to the student how much smoother the reading sounded as the rate increased.

5. To assure comprehension of the passage, ask the student a few questions about the content. You want the student to know that just because he is working on increasing his speed, you are also concerned with how much he understood.

Reference: Schreiber, 1980

A different way to approach repeat reading is to have the child try to read farther within a passage within a timed limit (usually one minute). When using this technique, you will need a timer that counts down to one minute and rings when the minute is reached. The goal is to have the student get farther in the passage each time with fewer errors. This is a very easy way to determine WPM since the number of words the student reads is the WPM. You can also give the student a words correct per minute (WCPM) score by deducting the number of errors. To make this task easier, I've included numbers that indicate the word counts for the passages in this book. They appear as superscript numbers in 25-word increments. The total number of words appears at the end of the passage. For more information, see **Word Count** in Appendix A on page 132.

1. Have the student read the passage while you time the baseline reading. Use a highlighter to mark any errors. If the student makes too many errors (more than 5% for independent level or 10% for instructional level), choose another passage. Discuss any words the student missed.

2. After the baseline reading, set the timer for one minute and tell the student to read the passage again, this time as quickly as he can. Let him know that if he makes an error, you will say the word correctly. You can decide if you want the student to repeat the word correctly before going on with reading. During the reading, if the student makes an error, immediately say what the word should have been. If the student makes a major error, you can turn off the timer to discuss what was wrong with the word and then continue the timed reading. It's important to count each error as it occurs. Use any method you choose to help you remember the total number of errors, such as making a mark on the corner of the passage or counting on your fingers. Another suggestion is to make two copies of the passage. As the student reads from one, you can use the other to note any errors. Write a small "B" above each error the student makes during baseline reading, a "1" for each error on the first reading after the baseline, etc. In this way, you can review all of the errors with the student.

3. When the timer goes off indicating that a minute has passed, mark the last word the student read. Ask him what his goal is for the next reading. How much farther does he think he can read and how many errors can he eliminate? Then reset the timer and have the student read for one minute again. Follow the guidelines described above. At the end of the minute, record the number of words the student read and the number of errors he made. Have the student set word and error goals for the next reading and repeat.

4. Praise the student for how much farther in the passage he has read each time. Discuss how the errors have decreased. Give the student a list of any words he consistently had difficulty with so he can practice them later. Point out to the student how much smoother the reading sounded as the rate increased.

5. To assure comprehension of the passage, ask the student a few questions about the content. You want the student to know that just because he is working on increasing his speed, you are also concerned with how much he understood.

Photocopy this sheet and fold it along the dotted line to make a tent. Fold the sheet so that the blank side of the paper is on the inside and the picture is on the outside. As you're working with a student on repeat reading, set the tent on the table with the picture facing the student to discourage him from guessing at words as he reads.

Name _____   Date _____

Today I used Repeat Reading technique:

Echo _____   Sprint _____   Sprint + Drill _____   Sprint + Style _____

Baseline

   Time: _____      Errors: _____

Trial #1

   Time: _____      Errors: _____

Trial #2

   Time: _____      Errors: _____

Trial #3

   Time: _____      Errors: _____

Trial #4

   Time: _____      Errors: _____

Name _____   Date _____

Trial #4 WCPM

_____

Trial #3 WCPM

_____

Trial #2 WCPM

_____

Trial #1 WCPM

_____

Baseline #1 WCPM

_____

Sample Student Progress Chart for Repeat Reading

Appendix M

Student: *Olivia*

Date	Passage	Method/# words	Baseline time	Errors	WPM/WCPM	#1 time	Errors	WPM/WCPM	#2 time	Errors	WPM/WCPM	#3 time	Errors	WPM/WCPM	Words to practice or notes
3-5	A-7	S / 45	:78 seconds	4	34/30	:76 seconds	3	35/33	:65 seconds	2	41/39	:58 seconds	0	46/46	their
3-5	A-8	S+D / 79	3:30 / 210 seconds	12											new passage; too difficult
3-5	A-9	S+D / 68	1:45 / 105 seconds	5	38/36	1:20 / 80 seconds	1	51/50	1:12 / 72 seconds	0	56/56	1:01 / 61 seconds	0	66/66	The drill really helped her.
3-9 *	B(S)-3	CD / 1:00	56 words	3	56/53	59 words	2	59/57	64 words	0	64/64	66 words	1	66/65	

Echo (E)   Sprint (S)   Sprint + Drill (S+D)   Sprint + Style (S+S)   Count Down Method (CD)

* Note: When using this form to record results using the Count Down method, you will need to record the time (which is constant at 1:00) in the 3rd column instead of # words. Also, the number of words read should be recorded in the 4th, 7th, 10th, and 13th columns instead of time.

Student Progress Chart for Repeat Reading

Appendix N

Student: _____

Date	Passage	Method/ # words	Baseline time	Errors	WPM/ WCPM	#1 time	Errors	WPM/ WCPM	#2 time	Errors	WPM/ WCPM	#3 time	Errors	WPM/ WCPM	Words to practice or notes

Echo (E)   Sprint (S)   Sprint + Drill (S+D)   Sprint + Style (S+S)   Count Down Method (CD)

* Note: When using this form to record results using the Count Down method, you will need to record the time (which is constant at 1:00) in the 3rd column instead of # words. Also, the number of words read should be recorded in the 4th, 7th, 10th, and 13th columns instead of time.

# of words correct per minute

Student: *Sabrina*

Date	Trial	Passage Read	30	40	50	60	70	80	90	100	110	120	130	140	150
4/10	B	C(S)-1													
	1														
	2														
	3														
4/12	B	C(S)-2													
	1														
	2														
	3														
	2B	C(S)-3													
	1														
	2														
	3														
4/14	B	C(S)-4													
	1														
	2														
	3														
4/17	B	C(S)-5													
	1														
	2														
	3														
4/19	B	C(S)-6													
	1														
	2														
	3														

You can highlight a target reading rate range (see Appendices R and S on pages 158 and 159). You might select the range between the 50th and 75th percentiles. You could also select a specific target, such as 50 WCPM, and then a range around that target (e.g., 40 to 60 WCPM). For students for whom that is an unrealistic target, you might select the 25th percentile as the target and choose a range of 10 WCPM in either direction. When the student is in the target range on 2 to 3 consecutive baseline readings, you might select a harder level text. However, the student still needs to be 90 to 95% correct on the baseline reading. Record the number of words correct per minute on the baseline reading and each subsequent reading. See Appendix Q on page 157 for the formula to calculate WPM and WCPM.

In the example above, on 4/12, two separate passages were used. Also, on 4/19, the student achieved baseline reading in the target range. If this occurs on two more consecutive readings, try selecting a harder passage (but the student should still be able to read it with 90-95% accuracy).

Reading Fluency Chart for Repeat Reading

# of words correct per minute

Date	Trial	Passage Read	30	40	50	60	70	80	90	100	110	120	130	140	150

Student: _____

Formula for Computing Words Per Minute (WPM) and Words Correct Per Minute (WCPM)

An easy way to figure the words per minute (WPM) is to use the following formula:

Take the number of words read divided by the seconds needed to read the passage. This yields the number of words per second. Then multiply by 60 for the number of words per minute.

$$\boxed{} \div \boxed{} = \boxed{} \quad \textbf{x 60} = \boxed{}$$

words read   # seconds to read   # words/second   # words/minute

Example A: Student reads a 100 word passage in 1:35 (95 seconds).

$100 \div 95 = 1.05$ (words per second) x $60 = 63$ WPM

Example B: Student reads 100 word passage in 45 seconds

$100 \div 45 = 2.22$ (words per second) x $60 = 133$ WPM

This formula works with any number of words read.

Example C: Student reads a 225 word passage in 3:25 (205 seconds)

$225 \div 205 = 1.09$ (words per second) x $60 = 65$ WPM

An easy way to figure words correct per minute (WCPM) is described in the box below.

WCPM

If you're using the Count Down method for a fixed one-minute sample, use the following formulae:

Count the number of words read in one minute. Then subtract the number of errors in that minute to get the words correct per minute (WCPM).

$$\boxed{} - \boxed{} = \boxed{}$$

words read   # errors   # WCPM

If you're using the Count Up method and the time is greater than or less than a minute, you need to subtract the errors before computing the average.

$$\boxed{} - \boxed{} \textbf{ x 60} = \boxed{} \div \boxed{} = \boxed{}$$

words read   # errors   # seconds to read   # WCPM

Using the same information in Example C above and knowing that the student made five errors, the second formula works this way:

$225 - 5 = 220$ x $60 = 13{,}200 \div 205 = 64$ WCPM

	Curriculum-based norms in oral reading fluency for grades 2 through 5 (medians)							
			Fall		*Winter*		*Spring*	
Grade	Percentile	n*	WCPM**	n	WCPM	n	WCPM	SD*** of raw scores
2	75	4	82	5	106	4	124	**39**
	50	6	53	8	78	6	94	
	25	4	23	5	46	4	65	
3	75	4	107	5	123	4	142	**39**
	50	6	79	8	93	6	114	
	25	4	65	5	70	4	87	
4	75	4	125	5	133	4	143	**37**
	50	6	99	8	112	6	118	
	25	4	72	5	89	4	92	
5	75	4	126	5	143	4	151	**35**
	50	6	105	8	118	6	128	
	25	4	77	5	93	4	100	

n*   = number of median scores from percentile tables of districts (maximum possible = 8)
WCPM** = words correct per minute
SD***   = the average standard deviation of scores from fall, winter, and spring for each grade level

From "Curriculum Based Norms in Oral Reading" by Jan E. Hasbrouck & Gerald Tindal, *Teaching Exceptional Children*, Spring 1992, pp. 41-44.
Copyright © 1992 by the Council for Exceptional Children
Reprinted with permission.

AIMSweb® Normative Data

Appendix S

		Fall		Winter		Spring		
Grade	%ile	Num	WRC	Num	WRC	Num	WRC	ROI
1	90	12140	49	51928	78	53723	106	1.6
	75		22		46		80	1.6
	50		8		23		52	1.2
	25		2		13		28	0.7
	10		0		6		15	0.4
	Mean		18		34		57	1.1
	StdDev		25		31		37	0.3
2	90	47914	103	45601	129	50868	143	1.1
	75		79		103		118	1.1
	50		54		77		92	1.1
	25		27		52		68	1.1
	10		14		25		42	0.8
	Mean		56		78		93	1
	StdDev		35		45		40	0.1
3	90	43969	130	42631	148	47706	163	0.9
	75		103		124		139	1
	50		77		96		110	0.9
	25		49		67		82	0.9
	10		30		41		52	0.6
	Mean		78		96		110	0.9
	StdDev		39		43		44	0.1
4	90	35769	149	37050	168	37689	184	1
	75		123		141		155	0.9
	50		99		114		126	0.8
	25		73		89		100	0.8
	10		48		62		73	0.7
	Mean		99		115		128	0.8
	StdDev		40		44		122	2.3
5	90	33720	169	35344	183	35579	198	0.8
	75		142		158		171	0.8
	50		112		128		141	0.8
	25		85		99		109	0.7
	10		60		73		82	0.6
	Mean		114		128		140	0.7
	StdDev		45		45		48	0.1
6	90	21457	182	22177	199	23551	211	0.8
	75		158		171		183	0.7
	50		131		144		155	0.7
	25		101		114		126	0.7
	10		70		83		94	0.7
	Mean		129		142		154	0.7
	StdDev		90		46		50	-1.1
7	90	12520	186	12015	197	13966	209	0.6
	75		160		169		183	0.6
	50		131		140		153	0.6
	25		103		112		124	0.6
	10		81		87		96	0.4
	Mean		132		141		153	0.6
	StdDev		42		44		45	0.1
8	90	10949	185	10701	193	12012	201	0.4
	75		162		170		180	0.5
	50		138		146		155	0.5
	25		107		115		127	0.6
	10		77		83		94	0.5
	Mean		134		141		152	0.5
	StdDev		42		45		47	0.1

Left margin: ROI = Rate Of Improvement WRC = Words Read Correct Num = Number of Students

This table is updated regularly. See www.AIMSweb.com for the most current data. Reprinted with permission from AIMSweb® (6/30/06).

Chapter 5
Reading Fluency and Comprehension

159

Copyright © 2006 LinguiSystems, Inc.

The activities in this chapter are designed to help improve the student's accuracy with better attention to the text and to improve prosody. Chapter 2 provides more detailed information about the areas that are addressed in this chapter:

▶ Inattention to orthography (O)
▶ Inattention to morphology (M)
▶ Inattention to serial order of words (SO)
▶ Inattention to self-monitoring of meaning (SM)
▶ Inattention to prosody (P)
▶ Inattention or lack of awareness of syntactic structure, including inattention to punctuation (SS)

Each activity in this chapter addresses one or more of these areas. Table 1 provides information detailing the types of activities and will help you decide which activities to use to work on specific target behaviors. A large, bold **X** means the activity is designed to address that skill. An * means the activity secondarily addresses that skill or skills as well, but you may need to point out to the student how that it is accomplished. You can address self-monitoring for meaning using any of the activities by simply stopping the student any time she makes an error and talking about whether what she has just read makes sense. That's why that skill is identified as either a primary or secondary target for all activities.

These activities are not "graded" because it is difficult to determine a grade level on a single sentence. You may decide to skip some of the stimuli in a specific activity if it seems inappropriate for the reading level of that student.

Table 1

Activity	Type of Activity	O	M	SO	SM	P	SS
1	Sentences with one word changed by orthography	**X**			*		
2	Sentences with one word changed by morphology		**X**		*		
3	Sentences with one word out of order			**X**	*		
4	Sentences with one-word changes	*	*		**X**		
5a	Stories to pull through a chunking machine				*	**X**	
5b	Dialogues				*	**X**	*
6a	Run-on sentences	*	*		*	*	**X**
6b	Sentences with punctuation changes				*	**X**	**X**

One word in each sentence has an orthographic change that makes it incorrect (e.g., a consonant or a vowel has been changed, resulting in another real word). Have the student read each sentence and find the mistake. Then have the student read the sentence again correctly. Discuss how a little change like this can disrupt the meaning of a sentence.

1. We took a long wide down the mountain.

2. My best friend and I love to skim in the creek.

3. The figs were oinking loudly in the barnyard.

4. When I failed the best, I was very sad.

5. Mom and Dad took all of us to the baseball same.

6. You should go see the ice skaters at the perk.

7. The sin was shining brightly when we were at the beach.

8. The strong wind helped me to keep my bite up in the air longer.

9. Our dog seeds to have a bath tomorrow.

10. As the sun came out, the show started to melt.

11. I made my cousin a get-well cord and gave it to him at the hospital.

12. Eva likes to read comic hooks when she is on vacation.

13. I got a punk balloon for my birthday because that is my favorite color.

14. Why are the dots chasing the cat in the backyard?

15. When Tom went to the store, he bought a new blue hot.

16. Lisa got a good graze in math on her school report card.

17. Pepperoni pizza is my favorite mood that my mom makes for dinner.

18. The principal fold Michael to be nice to his brother.

19. I like to play basketball, but I don't lake to play soccer.

20. Why are the hallways in the mouse painted green?

One word in each sentence has a morphological change that makes it incorrect (e.g., verb tense, comparative ending). Have the student read each sentence and find the mistake. Then have the student read the sentence again correctly. Discuss how a little change like this can disrupt the meaning of a sentence.

1. The horse run fast when the farmer opened the stable.

2. Why is he uses his old ball instead of the new one?

3. Where is the new playground that were built yesterday?

4. My dog jump high over the fence into the backyard.

5. I am going with my mom to visits Grandma on Thursday.

6. Mary drove me to school in her new car the morning.

7. Why are the kids next door played baseball?

8. Why didn't you come help me carry the strawberries I pick?

9. The turtle is slow than the fox.

10. At my soccer game this morning, I score a goal for the team.

11. When Mom drove to the mall, he decided to stop for ice cream.

12. Emily's new bike is smallest than her old one.

13. Eric brings his pet lizard to school last Friday.

14. I am very happier about all the presents I got for my birthday!

15. I drunk too much juice today and it made my stomach hurt.

16. Is Tyler actually going to wears that to the dance?

17. Our school picture was taking by the photographer.

18. I become friends with the new girl in my dance class.

19. Saint Patrick's Day is Monday, so I have to wore my green shirt.

20. Can we plans a party for next Friday night?

These sentences will help the student understand the importance of paying attention to word order when she reads. The first sentence in each pair has a word out of order. The second sentence is correct. Have the student read the first sentence and find the word that is out of order. Then have the student read the second sentence in the pair with the correct word order. If the student reads the first sentence correctly (i.e., unconsciously moves the word to the right spot), point out what she has done.

1. After the meeting I my met mother to have lunch.
   After the meeting I met my mother to have lunch.

2. Kelly and Brian went at shopping the mall on Tuesday.
   Kelly and Brian went shopping at the mall on Tuesday.

3. I had a wonderful time on my to trip Florida last summer.
   I had a wonderful time on my trip to Florida last summer.

4. Who did you ask to go to the dance with on you Friday?
   Who did you ask to go to the dance with you on Friday?

5. Jason moved to Wisconsin during summer of the 1998.
   Jason moved to Wisconsin during the summer of 1998.

6. When went we ice skating, Lucy fell and broke her arm.
   When we went ice skating, Lucy fell and broke her arm.

7. Who will feed the dog we when are gone on Friday night?
   Who will feed the dog when we are gone on Friday night?

8. The leaves on the turn trees a very beautiful color during fall.
   The leaves on the trees turn a very beautiful color during fall.

9. Kentucky becomes warm very and humid during the summer.
   Kentucky becomes very warm and humid during the summer.

10. Mark and I went sailing our on friend's boat on Saturday afternoon.
    Mark and I went sailing on our friend's boat on Saturday afternoon.

11. I had to a read biography of Thomas Jefferson for English class.
    I had to read a biography of Thomas Jefferson for English class.

12. He studied so much for his math that test he got the best grade in the class.
    He studied so much for his math test that he got the best grade in the class.

13. Each person should only one eat slice of pizza so there's enough for everyone.
    Each person should only eat one slice of pizza so there's enough for everyone.

14. My mother and father were very pleased they when received my report card.
    My mother and father were very pleased when they received my report card.

These sentences will demonstrate to the student how a sentence's meaning can change when only one word is altered. Have the student read each pair of sentences and then tell how they differ.

1. The apple I had for lunch was crunchy.
   The banana I had for lunch was crunchy.

2. Larry had a sore arm from playing volleyball.
   Larry had a sore leg from playing volleyball.

3. Jack plays football after school.
   Jack plays football before school.

4. The summer wind is blowing hard.
   The summer wind is blowing softly.

5. My favorite song is "Singing in the Rain."
   My favorite song is "Singing in the Snow."

6. Apple pie was for dessert after dinner.
   Apple pie was for dessert after breakfast.

7. The sugar cookies tasted delicious.
   The oatmeal cookies tasted delicious.

8. I ran down the street to go to the movies.
   I ran down the street to go to the store.

9. The weather forecast for tomorrow is sunny and hot.
   The weather forecast for tomorrow is rainy and hot.

10. Jack's cat is black and white.
    Jack's hamster is black and white.

11. The oven was hot when I touched it.
    The oven wasn't hot when I touched it.

12. The pig slept in the mud next to the barn.
    The pig stood in the mud next to the barn.

13. Leah set her alarm clock for 7:00 in the evening.
    Leah set her alarm clock for 7:00 in the morning.

14. I watched the artist draw a picture of a beautiful sunrise.
    I watched the artist draw a picture of a beautiful sunset.

15. The garage sale next door started at 2:00.
    The garage sale next door ended at 2:00.

The use of a chunking machine, or tachistoscope, is described in Chapter 2 on page 25. On pages 166-180, there are two stories from each grade level that have been formatted to work with a chunking machine. Cut a window in a 4"x6" index card so that it allows the student to only see one phrase at a time. The diagram below shows how it will look. Have the student read each phrase smoothly, not word-by-word. You can control the pace by how fast you move the index card down the page. After the student has read the phrases several times with the chunking machine, have her read the same story as it's printed in regular format in Chapter 5 to see if she can apply what she has practiced in terms of phrasing.

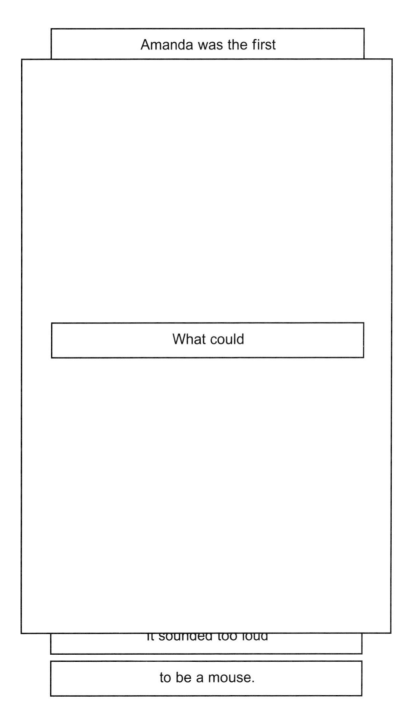

Amanda was the first

What could

It sounded too loud

to be a mouse.

Sequential Passage 1: Mac and Bell Dig a Hole

Mac and Bell	They decide to go
live in	under the fence.
a big house	Mac and Bell
with a big yard.	start to dig.
There is	They dig and dig
a big fence	all day long.
all the way	Finally the hole
around the yard.	is big enough,
There is a dog	and they go under!
in the next yard	Mac and Bell
named Sam.	play with Sam.
Mac and Bell	They chase
want to play	Sam's ball.
with Sam.	They jump
Mac and Bell	in Sam's pond.
can't jump	They even roll
over the fence.	in Sam's grass.

Sequential Passage 7: Mac Takes Bell's Toy

Bell has	When he eats,
a special toy.	he puts the frog
He likes it	by his bowl.
the best.	One day
It is	Bell is fast asleep.
an old green frog.	Mac sees the frog
It croaks	on the grass
when he bites it	beside Bell.
on the head.	Mac sneaks over.
Bell takes the toy frog	He bites the frog
with him	on its leg.
when he goes outside.	It does not
He sleeps	make a sound.
with the frog.	Then Mac runs away
	as fast as he can.

Non-Sequential Passage 2: Muffy Climbs a Tree

Muffy gets
out of the house.
She runs fast
to a big tree
she sees in the yard.
She climbs the tree.
She is up high
and can see far away.
She wants to come down,
but she cannot get down.
She cries and cries
until a girl hears Muffy
and comes to the tree.
The girl will help Muffy.

Non-Sequential Passage 3: Snake in the Grass

Becky is outside
without shoes
running in the grass.
She steps on something
that moves away fast.
Becky looks down
and sees a snake.
She yells very loudly
and points at the grass.
Her sister Jane comes
to see why
Becky is yelling.
Jane starts to yell too.
The girls run back
into the house.
Becky puts on her shoes
before she goes back out.

Non-Sequential Passage 1: Smoky Mountains

Harry and his family	When his dad
were going on a vacation,	cooked on the grill,
and he and his sisters	the backyard sometimes got smoky,
were sitting	and when he went
in the back of the van.	to his grandpa's house
Harry was stuck	and they burned leaves,
sitting between his sisters	the air got smoky.
because the girls always fought	But smoky mountains?
if they sat	Just then
next to each other.	Harry looked
His dad told him	out the front window
they would soon be	of the van
driving through	and saw the mountains ahead.
the Smoky Mountains.	It really did look like
Harry thought that seemed	there was smoke
like a strange name for mountains.	all around them.
	It turns out that Smoky
	was the perfect name
	for the mountains.

Non-Sequential Passage 4: The Birthday Party

Amanda went to the mailbox	Amanda's heart
and brought the mail	beat a little faster
into the house.	as she opened the card
She did this	to see who sent it.
almost every afternoon	She couldn't believe her eyes!
when she got home from school,	She was invited
but today	to a party for Mindy
something was different.	this Saturday.
Today there was an envelope,	Mindy was the most popular girl
pink with yellow and green candles	in the class.
around the edges,	Amanda would have to
addressed to her!	ask her mother
Amanda tore open the envelope,	to take her shopping
pulled out the card,	before Saturday.
and saw the words	
"You Are Invited"	
printed across the front of it.	

Non-Sequential Passage 4: Russ Helps the Family Pack

It had been	when you went outside,
another dismal year	making you close your eyes
for Russ and his family	and feel your way around.
in Oklahoma	Now the family
where his father	was moving back to Tennessee
was a farmer	where they could stay
who tried to grow corn and wheat.	with Russ's grandfather.
The attempt was not successful, however,	Russ helped his father
because for the second year	lift the last chair
in a row,	onto the back of the truck,
nothing grew.	and then they put the boxes
The crops of all the farmers	with the pots and pans in too.
in the region had died	His mother carried out some blankets
because it never rained,	and his baby sister
and the ground was as dry	who was scared and crying.
as it had ever been.	The heavy woolen blankets
The crops could not be expected	went into the back of the truck
to survive	before the whole family
in such dire conditions.	crowded into the front seat
Dust blew into your eyes	for the long and dusty drive
	back East.

Non-Sequential Passage 5: Liz Dreams Big

Things were quite different	of that day.
for girls in the 1800s	These jobs
compared to girls	were never Elizabeth's choice
going to school	when she pretended to be an adult, though.
in the 21st century.	Whenever she played pretend,
More than a century ago,	she chose to be a doctor,
girls were not permitted	perhaps because her grandfather
to do many things	was a doctor.
that boys could do,	Elizabeth loved to travel with him
though they were certainly capable.	when he visited his patients,
Elizabeth and her friends	and she even had a little black case
loved to pretend	that her grandfather had given her.
they were grown up.	In it she had collected
When they did this,	what she considered to be
some of Elizabeth's friends	some things doctors might use.
pretended to be teachers or shopkeepers,	She had the old bottles from pills
bankers or seamstresses.	and even some scissors and a saw
These were occupations	he no longer used,
that were currently held by women	though she didn't really want to know
and were familiar to the young girls	what the saw was for.

Passage 1: Floods

Water falls from clouds	There are two
and is absorbed in the soil	basic types of floods.
or fills rivers.	In a regular flood,
Then it evaporates	a river gets fuller and fuller
and returns to the clouds.	and then overflows its banks.
Floods occur	The more dangerous type of flood
when there is too much water	is a flash flood.
in the soil and rivers.	This occurs
Lots of things	when a wall of water
can cause this imbalance.	quickly sweeps
Heavy rainfall	over an area of land.
or lots of snow melting	Up until now,
can cause too much water	scientists haven't been very good
to build up in lakes, rivers, and streams.	at predicting when and where
Soil that is already too saturated	flash floods will occur.
from heavy rain	This is changing
can't hold any more water.	because of a tool
	called Doppler radar.

Chapter 6
Reading Fluency and Comprehension   **173**

Passage 6: Lightning

There doesn't need to be	A car with a metal roof
a major storm	also offers protection,
for lightning to strike.	as long as you are not touching
Lightning may be pretty	any metal part of the car
to look at,	that leads to the outside.
but it can be deadly.	Do you know the 30/30 rule
Lightning in the United States	for staying safe around lightning?
kills almost a hundred people a year.	If you see lightning,
The best place to be	count the seconds
during a lightning storm	until you hear thunder.
is inside a building.	If the number is 30 seconds or less,
However, even inside a building	you should go inside.
you have to be careful.	Stay there until 30 minutes
You should not be near	after the last thunder or lightning flash.
windows or doors,	
phone lines or power lines.	

Passage 5: Hillary Rodham Clinton

A modern-day First Lady,	She served prominent roles
Hillary was often as visible	during Bill's term as president.
as the president.	She chaired the Task Force on
She had her own career	National Health Care Reform.
before she married Bill.	She received some criticism
She was an excellent student and a leader	for her visible role.
involved in student government.	She was a strong supporter
After graduating from law school,	of women's and children's rights.
she worked for a while	She wrote a best-selling novel.
in Boston and Washington, D.C.,	It is entitled
before moving to Arkansas.	*It Takes a Village.*
There she married Bill	She also won a Grammy
and worked as a lawyer	for her recording of this book.
and taught in law school.	After Bill left office,
After he became governor,	Hillary became the first First Lady
she balanced her duties	elected to the United States Senate.
as Arkansas' First Lady	
with her public service work.	

Passage 6: Julia Dent Grant

Perhaps the most interesting part	He tried many business ventures
of Julia Grant's life	in St. Louis,
was the period before Ulysses	none of them successful.
assumed the presidency.	The Grants then returned to Illinois.
Julia and Ulysses,	Ulysses worked for his father
who was in the army,	in a leather goods store.
became engaged in 1844.	The Grants might have lived
However, they had to wait four years	the rest of their lives there,
through the Mexican War	but the Civil War began.
before they could marry.	Ulysses was called to duty.
After their marriage,	Once more,
Julia followed Ulysses	Julia was apart from her husband.
to many military posts.	She tried to meet him
She had to return home	when she could.
in 1852	After living such a hard life,
when he was sent to the West.	it must have been a wonderful time
He resigned from the army	for Julia serving as First Lady.
two years later	
to be with Julia and their children.	

Passage 5: Gloria Steinem

Gloria has an interesting start	She was politically active in college.
to her childhood.	After graduating,
She credits these experiences	she went to India
in helping her form her views of life.	to study for two years.
Gloria did not attend school	When she returned,
until she was 12 years old.	she could not find a job as a journalist
Instead, she traveled around the country	because editors wanted to hire men.
with her parents	She became a freelance writer.
in a house trailer	As a writer, she covered
as they bought and sold antiques.	political campaigns, among other things.
They believed this travel and exposure	She became active
to different parts of the country	in the feminist movement.
were as educational as any school.	She was a co-founder
When she was enrolled in school,	of the National Women's Political Caucus.
she found the adjustment difficult.	In 1972,
Gloria attended college	she founded the feminist magazine Ms.
on a scholarship.	

Passage 9: Benjamin Franklin

Benjamin Franklin	He invented the lightning rod
had three distinct careers	and lightning bells
in his lifetime.	while studying electricity.
He had success in the publishing business	He was lucky not to be killed
before he ever turned to science.	during any of his experiments
He started working as an apprentice	with lightning.
in his brother's printing shop	Perhaps because he understood
when he was only 12 years old.	the relationship between electricity and fire,
He loved to read.	he started the first fire insurance company
Once he tried to save money for books	in America.
by eating only vegetables.	He finished his life as a statesman.
At age 23,	He was appointed
he was publishing a newspaper.	to the first Continental Congress.
It was the first	He was instrumental
to use political cartoons.	in drafting the Declaration of Independence.
When he retired from printing	At age 81,
at age 39,	though quite frail,
he focused his interest in science.	he signed the Constitution of the United States.

Passage 4: Wilma Rudolph

Wilma Rudolph's incredible accomplishment	Her mother, a determined woman,
of being the first American woman	drove her 50 miles away for treatment
to win three gold medals.	to the black medical college
in the Olympics	of Fisk University in Nashville.
is more remarkable	She did this for two years,
knowing what Wilma had to overcome.	until Wilma was able to walk
She was born during the Great Depression	with the aid of a metal leg brace.
to a poor family in Tennessee,	By the time Wilma was 12,
the 20th of 22 children!	she could walk normally.
She was born prematurely	It was then that she decided
and weighed less than five pounds.	to become an athlete.
However, she could not be treated	In high school,
at the segregated hospital in town.	she was a basketball star
As a child,	before going to college
she had one illness after another,	and becoming a track star.
from mumps, scarlet fever, and chickenpox	She competed in her first Olympic games
to double pneumonia.	when she was 16 years old.
The she was told she had polio	
and that she would never walk again.	

Passage 6: Peggy Fleming

Peggy is credited	This was the first time the Olympics
with the revival of figure skating	were broadcast live and in color.
in the United States	The graceful young skater
after a tragic accident.	in the green dress
In 1961,	captivated those watching.
when Peggy was only 11 years old,	Peggy won the gold medal
the entire United States Figure Skating team	by an incredible 88 points
was killed in a plane crash	over the silver medalist.
on its way to the world championships.	Peggy's was the only gold medal
Those who died in the crash	the U.S. team won that year
included Peggy's skating coach	at the Winter Games.
and most of her role models.	Peggy went on to star in
For a while after the tragedy,	many television specials about skating,
Peggy didn't even feel like skating.	bringing the sport to the forefront.
However, she was determined	Four different White House administrations
to be a champion	invited her to visit.
and proved herself to be one many times over.	In 1980,
She won five U.S. titles	she became the first skater
and three World titles	invited to perform there.
leading up to the 1968 Olympics.	

Chapter 6
Reading Fluency and Comprehension　　　　**180**

Having students read brief dialogues can help them with prosody. Most conversations don't include vocabulary that is grade specific. Likewise, there are generally no lengthy sentences in dialogues. Since most readability formulae use length of sentence as one of the parameters for determining grade level, the dialogues in this activity are not graded. They also do not have character names, and thus, are gender-neutral for the most part. There are occasional references to *he* and *she* when it was unavoidable.

Select one of the six dialogues. Read the dialogue aloud to the student and help her with any possible difficult words. Then have the student choose which character she would like to portray. You be the other character. You may even want to use a highlighter to highlight the lines for each character (e.g., character 1's lines are highlighted in yellow, character 2's lines are blue). It's often a good idea after the first reading for you and the student to switch characters and reread the dialogue. That way, the student has heard you modeling the correct intonation and phrasing.

Dialogue 1
Scene: Two students cleaning up the art room after school
1 Tell me again why you volunteered us to stay after school.
2 Because we both need the extra points on our grade. At least I know that I do.
1 Ugh! You're right. If I bring home a C in art, my dad will positively flip out.
2 Hand me those paintbrushes, will you? I'll wash those while you sweep the floor.
1 What were they doing in last period? There's construction paper everywhere.
2 I bet they were making a collage. We did that last year, remember?
1 Yeah. Where's the trash can? I thought it was always back here by the windows.
2 How would I know? Do I have eyes in the back of my head?

Dialogue 2
Scene: Two children riding in the backseat of a car
1 How long did your mom say it would take to get there? I'm getting hungry.
2 I think we have about 45 minutes to go. I'm starving too! Hey, there's a box of cookies under the seat.
1 Well, get them out. Don't let your mom see us or we'll get the "don't eat now or you'll ruin your dinner" speech.
2 Really, does every mom in the world say that?
1 Shh! She'll hear you.
2 No she won't. She's listening to that radio station she likes. We could clap our hands and she wouldn't notice.
1 My mom listens to that too. Boring!

Dialogue 3
Scene: Two students talking outside school one morning
1 Did you see Henry this morning?
2 No, what's going on?
1 He got a haircut this weekend and he really did it.
2 Did what?
1 He dyed his hair blue right down the middle. I can't believe his mother let him do that.
2 Well, he's wanted to dye it for a really, really long time. He's such a Wildcat fan; you knew it would be blue, didn't you?
1 I can't wait until you see him. It's wild! His hair is so short on the sides, but long in the middle, and that's where it's blue.
2 Let's go. I bet he's at the lockers right now.

Dialogue 4
Scene: Two students waiting for band practice to start
1 These daily practices are really getting me down.
2 You're right, but it's only two more weeks until the competition. After that, Mr. Perry said we'd go back to practicing only twice a week.
1 I know, but two more weeks? I think my fingers will fall off before we get to the competition. My hands are so sore, I can hardly stand it.
2 Well at least your instrument doesn't weigh a ton. Try hauling around a tuba.
1 Hey, you chose it. Now you're stuck with it!
2 Don't remind me. I don't know what I was thinking.
1 Maybe you were thinking that no one else was trying out for tuba and you were bound to be selected for the marching band.
2 Yep, there's that. I do get to see all the football games from the front row.

Dialogue 5
Scene: Three students at the tryouts for a play
1 I'm so nervous I can hardly stand it. I've just got to get that part.
2 What role are you trying for?
1 The older sister. She doesn't have a lot of lines, I know, but I can really relate to the character. What about you guys?
2 Well, I thought maybe I'd try for the neighbor. He's so grumpy I thought it would be fun to play him. If not, maybe the coach.
3 Yeah, you'd be a funny neighbor. I don't want to have to memorize a lot of lines, so I'm going to try out for the crazy fan.
2 That character has lots of costume changes.
3 I know. I thought that would make the part interesting. Do you think we have to provide our own costumes?
1 No. When I did the play last year, the drama teacher asked the parents to bring in clothes we could use for costumes.
3 That's right. I forgot you were in the play last year.

Dialogue 6
Scene: Three people discussing a movie they just saw
1 Wow! That was awesome!
2 I think it was better than the first one, don't you?
3 Absolutely! I really thought Racer wasn't going to win that last race.
2 Yeah, especially when he rounded the last corner and came up over the hill. It looked like Chase was going to catch him.
1 I really don't like Chase. He didn't deserve to win.
3 Well of course not. But the good guy doesn't always win, you know.
1 Come on, how many movies have you seen where the villain wins? I bet you can't name one, can you?
2 I know one. Remember that movie we saw last summer? The one with the dragon?
3 Oh yeah, you're right. The hero did die at the end of that one, didn't she?

This activity is designed to show the student how important punctuation can be. Each practice item contains a run-on sentence that is two sentences written as one with a phrase at the boundary that could logically go with either sentence. For example, in the first item, the phrase "under the table" could refer to where the cat chased the ball or where the dog was sleeping. The examples that follow each run-on sentence (A and B) show the two ways the item could be punctuated. The first example is often the most logical, but either one is correct.

When working with a student, cover the page so that only the run-on sentence shows. Have the student read it all the way through. Ask her to identify two ways the run-on sentence could be punctuated. Then uncover examples A and B and have the student read them to see if she was correct. Talk about how the sentences changed due to the different punctuation.

1. My cat chased the ball under the table the dog was sleeping soundly.
   A. My cat chased the ball under the table. The dog was sleeping soundly.
   B. My cat chased the ball. Under the table, the dog was sleeping soundly.

2. The boy ran too fast at the park I like to swing on the swings.
   A. The boy ran too fast. At the park, I like to swing on the swings.
   B. The boy ran too fast at the park. I like to swing on the swings.

3. The monkeys at the zoo were swinging from the top of the tree they can see the lake.
   A. The monkeys at the zoo were swinging. From the top of the tree, they can see the lake.
   B. The monkeys at the zoo were swinging from the top of the tree. They can see the lake.

4. My new history teacher was very funny after school Jim and I like to play kickball.
   A. My new history teacher was very funny. After school, Jim and I like to play kickball.
   B. My new history teacher was very funny after school. Jim and I like to play kickball.

5. I fell and hurt my ankle on the playground last week cherry pie was served in the cafeteria.
   A. I fell and hurt my ankle on the playground. Last week, cherry pie was served in the cafeteria.
   B. I fell and hurt my ankle on the playground last week. Cherry pie was served in the cafeteria.

6. The birds flew in the garden butterflies were searching for nectar.
   A. The birds flew. In the garden, butterflies were searching for nectar.
   B. The birds flew in the garden. Butterflies were searching for nectar.

7. Eric bought the new movie that was released yesterday we all watched the movie after school.
   A. Eric bought the new movie that was released. Yesterday, we all watched the movie after school.
   B. Eric bought the new movie that was released yesterday. We all watched the movie after school.

8. At Maria's house, there are always cookies on Sunday we ate a dozen chocolate chip cookies.
   A. At Maria's house, there are always cookies. On Sunday, we ate a dozen chocolate chip cookies.
   B. At Maria's house, there are always cookies on Sunday. We ate a dozen chocolate chip cookies.

9. I like to watch figure skating on TV there are lots of shows about police.
   A. I like to watch figure skating. On TV, there are lots of shows about police.
   B. I like to watch figure skating on TV. There are lots of shows about police.

10. The squirrels run fast to climb up the tree in rainy weather I wear a raincoat.
    A. The squirrels run fast to climb up the tree. In rainy weather, I wear a raincoat.
    B. The squirrels run fast to climb up the tree in rainy weather. I wear a raincoat.

These sentences will help the student understand how attending to punctuation can help her read with expression and better understand the meaning of what she reads. Use a sheet of paper to cover the second sentence in each pair. Model reading the first sentence without any punctuation (i.e., read it without any pauses) or with the incorrect punctuation (e.g., a period instead of a question mark). Then uncover the second sentence in the pair and read it. Model how attending to the punctuation makes the sentence easier to understand and sound more natural. Sentences 1-10 have only one type of punctuation missing. Sentences 11-15 have more than one missing type. You may also use this activity to see if the student can tell where the punctuation belongs by only showing her the first sentence in each pair.

1. Henry the neighbor's dog crawled under the fence.
   Henry, the neighbor's dog, crawled under the fence.

2. My brother called the dog but the dog didn't hear him.
   My brother called the dog, but the dog didn't hear him.

3. Don't touch that.
   Don't touch that!

4. Thomas be careful on the ice.
   Thomas, be careful on the ice.

5. Can you believe how much homework we have.
   Can you believe how much homework we have?

6. The big heavy leather book was on the table.
   The big, heavy, leather book was on the table.

7. Susan B. Anthony an important woman in U.S. history worked to achieve the right for women to vote.
   Susan B. Anthony, an important woman in U.S. history, worked to achieve the right for women to vote.

8. The graph figure 4 will help you answer the last question.
   The graph (figure 4) will help you answer the last question.

9. My best friend a great tennis player injured his ankle and couldn't play.
   My best friend, a great tennis player, injured his ankle and couldn't play.

10. The football players have won only four games yet they hope to make the playoffs.
    The football players have won only four games, yet they hope to make the playoffs.

11. After school I have to do homework go to practice take out the garbage and call Bob.
    After school, I have to do homework, go to practice, take out the garbage, and call Bob.

12. Did you really think the teacher would go for a half baked idea like that.
    Did you really think the teacher would go for a half-baked idea like that?

13. More than anything Sonya said I want a new shiny red bike for my birthday.
    "More than anything," Sonya said, "I want a new, shiny, red bike for my birthday."

14. Grandpa needs help with the following cleaning the garage washing the car and mowing the lawn.
    Grandpa needs help with the following: cleaning the garage, washing the car, and mowing the lawn.

15. Cats dogs birds and rabbits spilled out of the house as Josh shouted come back here.
    Cats, dogs, birds, and rabbits spilled out of the house as Josh shouted, "Come back here!"

23-06-987654321